To Maria
very warm regards
Brée

To Lea

Preface

*The material in this book is primarily the result of our frustrations and successes in attempting to create an empowered organization. It is also the result of more than 12 years of experience in assisting organizations, both in the United States and abroad, in facilitating the process of empowerment. The good news is the process works! The bad news is it is a long-term, challenging process. We believe that no matter how challenging and difficult the process, empowerment is a necessity for the survival of most organizations around the world. In today's fast-paced, customer-oriented world, hierarchy simply does not work to meet the crucial expectations of **quality, speed, customization,** and **service**.*

This book is intended to clarify much of the mystery and confusion associated with empowerment. Replete with examples, you will undoubtedly begin to see yourself, your organization, and situations you can identify with in this text. Slowly but surely, the magnitude and power of empowerment will be reinforced. How-tos will be less necessary, and your natural abilities and inclinations will take over.

This book is a journey. At first, like any uphill climb, you may seriously wonder if it is going to be worth it or why you even started out in the first place. We encourage you to hang in there! From our own experience, when the fruits of your labor begin to manifest, there is no sweeter experience.

We come largely from our experience and we invite you to do the same. After all, that's what empowerment really is all about!

The Authors

EMPOWERMENT
For High-Performing Organizations

"The essence of empowerment is maximizing human potential, not simply delegating authority."

The Authors

William A. Guillory and Linda A. Galindo

The Empowerment Spiral

The cover design illustrates successive project cycles, beginning and ending at successive dots, represented by the solid line spirals. After each cycle, expanded empowerment occurs as represented by the ΔEs (see pages 106 to 107).

Cover design by Lila Cazayoux

First Printing, 1995
ISBN: 0-933241-09-7
Printed in the United States of America

Introduction

This text is divided into three major sections — *Personal and Organizational Empowerment, Teamwork,* and *Organizational Support System*. The first section defines empowerment, both in terms of the individual and the organization. It establishes the foundation upon which empowerment is based — personal responsibility, accountability, and empowerment. It further provides a three-step process for learning these crucial concepts as everyday working skills. The section concludes with a discussion of the relationship between personal empowerment and personal growth. We believe personal growth is at the heart of organizational transformation.

The second section is a discussion of teamwork and its importance to implementing *any* high employee-involvement initiative. We show that teamwork is central to the success of empowerment, particularly in meeting the demand for speed in creating and delivering products, goods, and services. In this section, we discuss the definition of *team empowerment*, diversity in teams, and how to systematically incorporate teamwork. We also provide tools and exercises from our seminars that can be invaluable in developing practical teaming skills.

The third section is a discussion of the organizational support system necessary to have empowerment become institutionalized. We discuss three essential components — *leadership, management commitment,* and an *empowerment infrastructure*. The organizational support system requires leadership and commitment. The challenge is not only to one's self in giving up control and delegating authority, but also not allowing the effort to stall and fail when the inevitable sources of resistance appear. For successful organizations, strong leadership is a necessity. For struggling organizations, the motivation is "we change or we go out of business." As you can surmise, the necessity for a new type of leader is emerging — one having courage and conviction to stay the course in a time of rapid and turbulent change *and* keep the organization successful!

This text is not intended to be an exhaustive treatise of empowerment. It is a discussion of philosophies, principles, and methodologies for implementing empowerment. Furthermore, based upon our experiences within our own organization and with clients, we know they work! We have weaved diversity throughout this text rather than treat it as a separate subject. We believe diversity and empowerment are inseparable, both in theory and practice. Personal stories are indicated as (BG) for Bill Guillory.

If you are a working practitioner of empowerment or high-involvement, then you can proceed to read the text in any way you find it most useful without having missed anything from previous chapters. Frankly, we like to skip around a book to get a feel for the message. On the other hand, if you are more methodical, then the discussions and applications are laid out in a logical manner.

We hope you gain value from and enjoy (in that order) our labor of love.

Bill Guillory
Linda Galindo

Contents

PART III   ORGANIZATIONAL SUPPORT SYSTEM

Acknowledgments

We acknowledge, most of all, our clients and employees who have taught us everything about this subject worth remembering and learning. We acknowledge our friends and colleagues who have contributed to this text in innumerable ways. We are grateful to John Giovale of W. L. Gore and Associates, Inc. of Flagstaff, Arizona, for all he has taught us about high employee involvement. One of the authors (William A. Guillory) would like to acknowledge his friend and mentor, Les Alberthal, as a constant source of inspiration and support in understanding the relationship between business and empowerment. We gratefully acknowledge Christine DelPrete of Deseret Moon Documentation, Inc. for the art design and figures throughout the text. We thank Melissa Egbert, Jan Nystrom, and Allycen Farnsworth who managed the production of this manuscript. They have spent countless hours as producers in bringing this text to reality. Finally, we thank our editor, Norma Anderson, for refinements and finishing touches.

Foreword

"Many organizations are working hard to change the way they have structured themselves. It has become apparent that there is considerably more potential for people to contribute to organizational success than is being realized in highly structured organizations. The authors, in their discussions of empowerment, are expressing ways of releasing the energies inherent in people to greatly influence the success of their organizations. Becoming an empowered individual and working with empowered teams not only can better serve the objective of the organization, but creates a working environment where people have fun and are personally invested in success."

John Giovale, Associate
W. L. Gore and Associates, Inc.

Part I.

Personal and Organizational Empowerment

There is no such thing as an empowered organization, without competent, self-managed, and continuously learning employees.

The Authors

Chapter 1. **Empowerment**

♦ Introduction

Empowerment is one of the most misunderstood buzzwords in today's business world. Everyone uses the term, but few of us seem to understand empowerment or how to implement it into our organizations. Without a clear definition and consistent education, we tend to live out what we *think* it means, thus creating the chaos that is often associated with empowerment when it is misunderstood.

The following example illustrates the confusion and dysfunction often associated with implementing empowerment when it is not clearly understood.

As the CEO of Data Systems, Inc. delivered his state-of-the-company address to the work force, his audience became visibly more attentive when he made his final pronouncement: "Competition is demanding that we change the way things are done. We are committed to our quality initiative and you are key to our success. You are empowered to do whatever it takes for us to be successful."

Harry, who had joined the company a year ago, thought "I wish you'd tell my manager that. I see a lot of things that could help this organization and if I offer even so much as a suggestion, I'm told it's always been done *this* way. If I try to rock the boat one more time, I'll be lucky to keep my job."

- Does the CEO need to clarify what he means by "You are empowered?"
- Is Harry's manager the problem?
- Does Harry have anything to do with the conflict he is experiencing with his manager?

What does *empowerment* mean anyway?

Empowerment is not the passengers flying the plane. Empowerment is not irresponsibly delegating authority or asking for everyone's input, all the time, on how the organization should be run. Most important of all, empowerment is not something we can *give* each other. Yet, here stands the CEO telling Harry and his colleagues, "You are empowered to do whatever it takes for us to be successful." Imagine a group of people hearing that message and without any further explanation, leaving the meeting to make it happen. Some may think it means they can do whatever they want and the boss needs to stop bugging them. Some may think the boss will make empowerment clear and give them an exact explanation that can be followed and rewarded. Still others leave as they came in, completely mystified and hoping that, whatever it means, it doesn't affect them. All too often, this is a common scenario when empowerment is introduced into an organization. When understood and properly implemented, however, empowerment can be a very powerful and important tool for an organization's success in today's highly competitive business environment.

In this chapter we will lay the groundwork for thinking about empowerment in a *radically* different way than is expressed in most books written about this subject. We invite you to stay with us as we navigate through these somewhat challenging but essential concepts that are at the heart of what this book is about. We will sequentially discuss the following: the definition of empowerment, the components of an empowered organization, implementing empowerment, and the key elements of an empowerment initiative.

◆ What Is Empowerment?

Empowerment is the capacity to perform — as individuals, teams, and organizations. It is a measure of the individual or collective ability to produce a product or service of value to someone. Although empowerment is difficult to measure directly, we infer its measurement by the continued success of an individual or organization. For example, few of us would disagree that Muhammad Ali was a very empowered individual. He combined a winning attitude with outstanding athletic skills to be an exceptional boxing champion.

The same is true of Helen Keller who overcame deafness and blindness. Coached by Anne Sullivan Macy, she learned braille and taught herself a way to hear and speak by feeling the vibrations in her throat. After graduating from Radcliffe College at twenty-four, she became a lecturer and writer, and raised money for the deaf and blind. In reflecting on her life, she is quoted as saying, *"Life is either a daring adventure or nothing!"*

An excellent example of an empowered organization is the Microsoft Corporation. It has experienced unprecedented success (for an organization its size) as a result of products of widespread appeal at competitive costs. An empowered individual or organization is most visibly measured by continued success in rapidly changing times.

◆ The Components of an Empowered Organization

Achieving an empowered organization requires the complementary efforts of two major components: an organizational support system and individual and team empowerment. An organizational support system consists of the practices, policies, and procedures which are facilitated by leadership and

3

management in order to ensure the effective implementation of empowerment. Individual and team empowerment refers to empowered employees. That is, employees who are *self-managed, highly competent,* and *continuously learning.* These are individuals whose performance justifies the delegation of job authority with the least amount of management oversight. Therefore, the basic unit necessary to implement empowerment is empowered employees.

◆ Implementing Empowerment

The process of implementing empowerment in a stepwise manner is illustrated by the following diagram:

Organizational Support System

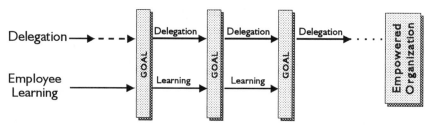

Empowered Employees

When most traditional organizations begin an empowerment initiative, the ability of the work force to perform independently is typically greater than the authority they have been delegated. This difference is illustrated by the differing lengths of the two (left side) solid arrows above. The difference in the lengths of the two arrows, indicated by the dotted portion, represents the extent to which employees can competently perform but are not delegated authority to do so. Therefore, when delegation is initially the major empowerment implementation activity, individuals and teams are being delegated tasks that they can already accomplish. It would appear that empowerment is working by simply delegating more authority.

It is when the two (left side) solid arrows become equal in length that the empowerment process really begins in earnest. At this point, management needs to delegate beyond what employees and teams have proven they can accomplish. In a like manner, employees need to successfully accomplish the expanded delegation they have been granted. This expanded delegation, by definition, will require new learning on the part of leadership, management, and employees. Leadership and management will be required to provide mentoring, coaching, support, and the sharing of power and control (upper arrows). Employees will be required to continuously learn new skills and competencies, how to manage and organize their jobs, and how to expand their sense of responsibility and accountability for their work (lower arrows). This is the *essence* of the progressive growth of empowerment.

The following scenario is a description of what commonly happens when an empowerment initiative is first attempted.

The results of an Empowerment Assessment at a local publishing company revealed that the work force was capable of more than they were being allowed to do. Counterproductive work force behaviors, including high absenteeism, an unwillingness to participate in organizational meetings, and "just getting by" now had an explanation. Recently, management had focused on reducing costs and improving efficiency. Management stressed the importance of individual initiative in continuous learning, working together with less necessity for being managed, and becoming more decentralized. Everyone began in earnest to carry out the new mandates, but when the time came for some individual managers to really "let go" where stretch projects were concerned, they found it more difficult than they thought it would be.

This example illustrates the challenge managers face when the two (left side) arrows are equal in length — the willingness to delegate beyond proven competency. This process must be done in a responsible way in order to be successful. Consequently, careful judgment of what employees can accomplish is a critical managerial skill. Substantive communication between managers and employees regarding the guidelines and performance expectations of the delegated authority is important. And finally, managers must ensure both the success of the project *and* the new learning by employees. These skills and competencies must be learned as an organization moves to greater organizational empowerment.

For example, in the implementation of its empowerment initiative, the ENSERCH Corporation developed the following guidelines for its leaders (organizational support system) and its employees (empowered employees).

Empowerment exists when:

LEADERS	EMPLOYEES
• Delegate sufficient authority for employees to do their jobs and satisfy their customers' requirements.	• Accept the responsibility to perform their jobs to the best of their abilities and to satisfy their customers' requirements.
• Communicate standards for employee performance and require performance against such standards.	• Accept the responsibility to achieve or surpass the performance standards for their jobs.

LEADERS	EMPLOYEES
• Encourage and make available skill development and training.	• Achieve their full potential by developing the skills to fully perform their responsibilities.
• Provide a supportive environment and constructive performance coaching.	• Provide input on work processes and broader issues.
• Seek and value employee input on both work processes and broader issues.	• Act as part of an overall company team and support the decisions of that team.
• Encourage informed risk-taking and proactive decision making, accepting honest mistakes without reprisal.	• Develop a sense of personal ownership of the business.

These guidelines illustrate how the two complementary components of an empowered organization play out in terms of the diagram shown on page 4.

Figure 1 is a description of the continuum which exists between hierarchical and self-management styles of operation. Superimposing the diagram shown on page 4 on Figure 1 shows that empowerment is best implemented in progressive steps corresponding to "responsible delegation" (upper short arrows) and "continuous learning" (lower short arrows). The extent to which an organization moves along this scale from left to right will be primarily determined by

7

three factors: the necessities of the business market, the commitment of leadership, and ultimately the willingness of the work force to demonstrate by performance that they accept the new reality.

Models of Management

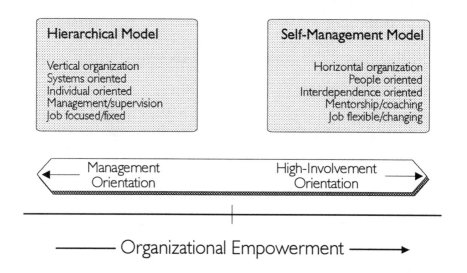

Figure 1.   Hierarchical self-management continuum corresponding to greater employee empowerment as high-involvement increases.

♦ The Elements of an Empowerment Initiative

The implementation of an empowerment initiative involves the synergism of three organizational elements:

1) The environment

2) The structure and systems
3) The process of implementation

The environment, and the structure and systems are the major responsibilities of leadership and management, respectively. Team and individual processes are the major responsibility of employees. The first two elements above refer to the organizational support system and the third element refers to empowered employees, both of which we discussed in the previous section.

A model which is used to clearly distinguish these three elements of an empowerment initiative is shown below:

{CONTEXT}   {CONTENT}   {EXPERIENCE}

Environment   **Structure and**   **Process**
                     System

Context characterizes the environment or climate. As a future state, it is usually described by a vision statement. When President Kennedy stated in his inaugural speech in 1960, "Ask not what your country can do for you; ask what you can do for your country," he was establishing a new context for U.S. Americans. When Jerry Junkins, the CEO of Texas Instruments, states "Our intention is to be a world-class organization," he is creating an environment where high performance is expected. Therefore, context is a description of what it is (or could be) like to be part of a change movement or to be part of a progressive organization. Leadership often communicates from this domain.

Content characterizes the description of the management structure and system, i.e., a flat structure and a high employee-involvement system. These elements may play

9

out by a matrix structure and a consensus management style. Management operates and communicates most often from this domain. It is a description of what is done in order to implement the empowerment initiative.

Experience characterizes the process of implementing an initiative by putting processes and procedures into practice. This element is exemplified by the extensive implementation of self-directed and high-performance teams. These activities require self-motivated and continuously learning individuals. Most employees operate from this domain by posing the question, "How do I (or we) do it?"

Using these three descriptions of context, content, and experience, the three elements of an empowerment initiative can be stated in the following manner:

1) The expectation of exceptional individual and team performance (context).

2) A high employee-involvement system within a decentralized structure (content).

3) Self-motivated employees who are committed to continuous learning (experience).

Think of it! Using this description of an empowerment initiative, all employees would experience an expectation that they perform in accordance with their capabilities, alone and with others. In addition, the organizational structure is no longer a hindrance because decisions are made closer to the point of contact with the customer. But best of all, individual responsibility and accountability for doing each and every activity right the first time is ingrained into the culture. This is the reality of organizational success for the

1990s and into the twenty-first century. The focus is on maximizing human potential as a necessity for achieving high performance. The power of this model is that it clearly defines all of the elements necessary to implement empowerment and describes who is responsible for performing each of them.

The following scenario is an example which illustrates the application of this model to an empowerment initiative played out by North American Semiconductors, Inc.

North American Semiconductors, Inc. experienced a shift to global competition almost overnight. To remain competitive, it was clear to the leadership that a new way had to be implemented to meet customer demands faster than the competition, while ensuring quality products.

Taking time out to examine the situation, the CEO came to some very clear conclusions designed to produce a return on stockholder investment. These conclusions would dictate future communication to her leadership team and to the organization.

1) **The Vision** - "An innovative, flexible organization focused on business processes which are responsive to exceeding customer needs." This vision is achieved when the following conditions are present:

   - An organization where mutual respect, integrity, open communication, and trust exist.

   - Employees have a passion for service, learning, and continuous improvement.

2) **The Principles** - The structure and system necessary to achieve an empowered organization include the following:

   - A structure which promotes the extensive dissemination and sharing of information.

- Initiatives which focus customers at the center of the business activities.
- A system of management which is organized for speed and responsiveness.
- A shift from control-oriented management to mentorship, coaching, and facilitating.
- A system which promotes participative leadership.

3) **The Process** - The overall process which drives the empowerment initiative toward the achievement of the vision includes activities which:

- Focus on creating customer partnerships.
- Are benchmarks that serve as the standards to exceed.
- Encourage, acknowledge, and reward outstanding individual and team performance.
- Promote individual and collective responsibility and accountability.

This example illustrates how the three major elements of an empowerment initiative are implemented. Though somewhat ideal in its description, it is actually taken from real examples of initiative statements from various Fortune 500 companies.

The vision, the principles, and the process are examples of context, content, and experience, respectively, as shown by the model on page 9. All three are vital elements which should be simultaneously implemented in order to achieve success.

This chapter has established the definition of empowerment, the components of an empowered organization, and the elements of an empowerment initiative. Building on these concepts, we can now define, in depth, an empowered organization. The excitement comes when we begin to see the possibility empowerment opens up to create a high-performance organization which is second to none.

Chapter 2. **The Empowered Organization**

◆ Introduction

Given the definition of empowerment we established in the first chapter, a major objective of this chapter is to show how empowerment is related to high performance. What we will discover is that all of the separate-looking, high-involvement initiatives that we have been instituting in the recent past have actually been part of a grand scheme to create a high-performance organization. The challenge facing us now is to integrate and institutionalize these initiatives into a single thrust. The integrating factor common to all high-involvement initiatives is empowerment. In this chapter, we discuss four topics: the definition of an empowered organization, the relationship between empowerment and success, why empowerment is a necessity for high performance, and the shift in mindset necessary for empowerment to work.

◆ What Is An Empowered Organization?

We stated in the previous chapter that an empowered organization is one that is continually successful. Success is measured not only in profitability, but also in terms of the professional growth and well-being of employees. Profitability is usually the result of meeting or exceeding the expectations of customers in four major areas: *quality, customization, speed,* and *service.*[1] Therefore, we define an empowered organization as one which continually delivers quality, customization, speed, and service while simultaneously achieving the professional growth and well-being of its employees. The first part of this definition characterizes the internal and external performance which assures efficient and profitable operation, respectively. The second part of this definition characterizes continuous learning by employees and the quality of work life they experience. When both components are working synergistically, success is virtually assured.

Quality

The first of the four areas which assure profitability is quality. Few consumers today will compromise on the quality of products and services they purchase — mainly because they do not have to. Given the extensive communication and distribution channels available, consumers can get virtually any product or service they desire from most parts of the world. Recognizing this fact, even discount and medium-price stores such as K-Mart, Wal-Mart, HomeBase, and J. C. Penney are stressing the quality of their products and friendly service. In addition to quality, consumers are also demanding products and services that are customized to their particular wants and needs.

Customization

Customization is the second area of profitability. It is driven not only by technological advancements, which allow the production of a great variety of goods and services, but also by recognition of the diverse marketplace. Fewer and fewer consumers want a product or service generated from a single mold. An expression which captures the response to this demand is, "You can have your burger your way." In the consulting business, there are few services customers appreciate more than seminars and supporting materials designed in a way which is unique to their organization — such as including their logo and examples of their experiences in the supporting materials. Customization is the result of having the patience to really understand customers' needs, and a willingness to go the extra mile to exceed their expectations. These efforts lead to a relationship of integrity which ultimately pays off in long-term dividends of continued business.

Customization is also the recognition and acknowledgment of the diversity of people. Consumers are keenly aware, in their buying habits, of how a product relates to them personally. For example, do the variety of dolls available represent the ethnic makeup of customers or the geographical base? Do children's books reflect the approximately one-third ethnic-minority population of the United States? Are the mannequins displaying clothes representative of its purchasers or at least ethnically neutral? A major cosmetics firm learned that 36 percent of its profits were from ethnic-minority customers and only 5 percent of its marketing budget targeted this population. A major producer of instant recyclable cameras discovered that while 100 percent of their cameras were produced and tested by men, 90 percent of their users were women. Examples such as these are endless. The point is simply that diversity and customization go hand in hand. They are inseparable.

Speed

Speed is the third area of profitability. It continues to be a major element of successful businesses. Fast-food businesses speak for themselves, when consumers want to get in and out with the least amount of time in lines. I (BG) recently attempted to purchase a book from a well-known chain store. The book I wanted was not in stock. They informed me that they could acquire it in three weeks. I decided to try another bookstore and had the same experience. Finally, I went home and called the publisher, and the book was sent to me in three days. They even offered to send it overnight if I would pay for postage.

The elements of speed and reliable service are the basis of alternative mail services such as Federal Express, Airborne Freight, UPS, DHL, etc. Speed in the dissemination of information, such as faxes and E-mail, is on the verge of a revolution created by advancements in information technology. The information highway has already begun to revolutionize marketing and sales. A sales organization for Adidas America, located in Portland, Oregon, makes extensive use of a Texas Instruments notebook computer and a management software program for organizing their sales transactions. Their data base contains more than 16,000 customers. The program is used to store and access customer information, schedule meetings, store conversations with customers and employees, send form letters and faxes, and a variety of other vital business activities. The point is the use of information technology allows anytime/anywhere access to customers and employees.

Speed will become increasingly important in maintaining a competitive edge in business. Areas where this will be particularly prominent are cycle time, development and delivery of new products, and response time to customer requests. All of these will have to be delivered in shorter time frames while maintaining a high standard of quality. As of this writing, both Federal Express and UPS have announced same-day mail service between the U. S., Canada, and Mexico. Finally, the success of a product is dependent upon how well it is delivered to the public in terms of service.

Service

Service is the fourth area of profitability. It begins with a mindset of commitment to the success of someone else. Exceptional service may often appear to be a personal sacrifice. This is rarely the case. The key to delivering exceptional service is seeing the world through your customers' eyes. The most common error we make in delivering service

to someone is to assume we know what is best for them —
even if they do not know! This is faulty judgment. Customers *always* ultimately know what is best for themselves. We
may provide information and experience for their consideration, but in the final analysis they know best. An unwillingness to acknowledge this reality means that a supplier
is more attached to his or her own ideas than in serving the
best interests of a customer. This conclusion relates both to
internal and external customers.

When we set aside our assumptions about what is best for
customers, we are open to learn what customers want and
need as seen through *their* eyes. This requires the setting
aside of our own opinions so that we might understand and
even empathize with their situations. This is actually an
act of humility which can be a breakthrough in understanding the true meaning of service. Then all of the how-tos we
have been taught or, more important, those we create, can
really become useful. Without this shifted perspective, they
are of limited usefulness. But with this shifted perspective
we can probably come up with much more uniquely designed ways of serving customers than those that others
provide for us.

In addition to the focus on the four areas relating to
profitability and internal productivity, empowered organizations operate consistent with the expression, "People are our
most valuable resource." This expression is reflected in
opportunities for professional growth through continuous
learning and employee well-being by their experience of
quality of work life.

Professional Growth

Continuous learning is the source of professional growth. Continuous learning really begins with the changing needs of customers. As customers require better and faster products and services uniquely designed for their needs, we respond by supplying them. Quite often, supplying their changing needs requires us to learn new skills and competencies. It is important to understand that continuous learning is driven by customer demands and not by leadership and management simply believing it is a good idea. Where employees are not in direct contact with customers, leadership and management must play the role of ensuring that employees adapt to the changing marketplace. The net result of continuous learning is that an empowered organization continues to get better at what it does.

Sometimes getting better might involve a radically different direction in terms of the products and services an organization produces. This situation is particularly true during rapidly changing times. For example, as a result of the Strategic Arms Limitation Treaty (SALT) with the former U.S.S.R., many of the DOE- and DOD-supported facilities have shifted their focus to consumer products, environmental programs, and technology transfer. The success these organizations experience will be measured by their levels of organizational empowerment. Those facilities that make a successful transition to the needs of the rapidly changing times are more empowered than those that do not. Thus, an empowered organization is not only able to adapt to change in terms of activity, but has employees who are equally willing to shift their thinking and competencies. The greatest challenge, by far, is the shift in mindset to service and customer orientation to which profit-making businesses have been traditionally subjected. The issues of competency and performance are unquestioned. Employees in these facilities are among the brightest in our society, if not the world.

Employee Well-Being

Everything we have discussed so far regarding an empowered organization is held together by how well employees perceive they are treated — more specifically, employees' experience of quality of work life. This aspect is often underestimated or inadvertently overlooked in terms of employee commitment and productivity. Elements of quality of work life include the opportunity for creativity, self-motivation, self-management, pride in work, organizational inclusion, loyalty, and self-actualization. These elements can be directly related to the bottom line in terms of individual and organizational productivity, continuous quality improvement, self-directed teams, and the overall physical and mental health of employees.

Organizations that operate in an overly stressful way experience high absenteeism, increased health care costs, and consistent quality breakdowns. Processes are often repeated because products and services are not done right the first time. Environments which foster self-motivation, self-management, and creativity, nurture employees who can solve problems without the need for management, organize and execute their own work, and are usually first to market with new products and services. Very little impacts the bottom line more than how these elements play out in an organization's operation.

Now that we know what an empowered organization is, how empowered does an organization have to be in order to be successful?

◆ How Empowered Must an Organization Be in Order to Be Successful?

Figure 1 on page 8 illustrates how an organization can become more empowered. That is, it becomes more empowered by the progressive movement of its work force toward the characteristics of the high-involvement model: horizontal organization, people oriented, interdependence oriented, mentorship/coaching, and job flexibility/changing. Movement to the right of this continuum is achieved by the continuing professional growth of employees in three areas: self-management, competence, and continuous learning. These are also the three criteria we used in defining an empowered employee.

The extent to which an organization has to move along the continuum of Figure 1 in order to become more empowered, by the definition in the previous section, is variable. In other words, no one definition describes an empowered organization in terms of how an organization is structured or managed. The real objective of empowerment is posed by the question, how far do we have to move along the continuum of Figure 1 in order to be an empowered organization? If 70 percent is the answer, then, on average, the organizational operation should be an *integration* of 70 percent high-involvement characteristics and 30 percent management characteristics. If the answer is 40 percent, the operation should be an integration of 40 percent high-involvement characteristics and 60 percent management characteristics. High-involvement and management characteristics correspond to the right and left side descriptions of Figure 1, respectively.

By using this integrated approach, an organization has available the entire spectrum of operation illustrated by Figure 1, and the flexibility to use the most effective approach suitable to the situation. In other words, some degree of management is not only necessary, but in some cases desirable (left side, Figure 1). In a like manner, there are inevitable situations where processes are best determined and improved by those closest to the work (right side, Figure 1). The utilization of the entire management continuum, according to the situation, is what we define as systems diversity (pages 206-07).

For a manufacturing organization to be empowered may require structured processes which are well managed. It may also require the extensive utilization of teamwork. Examples of this type of operation are the production of tennis shoes, personal computers, or automobiles. These types of operations may require only 40 percent self-management characteristics in order to be successful. On the other hand, a company which creates software programs or information technology requires a much greater level of employee empowerment. Most of the employees have to manage their own projects, be extremely creative, solve their own problems, and achieve all of these in an increasingly shorter time frame. As technology continues to reshape how work is performed, more and more jobs are requiring employees with highly technical skills. Therefore, high-performing employees will be an expectation of employers as we move through the remainder of this decade. If high performance is the key to future success, what is its relationship to empowerment?

♦ The Relationship Between Empowerment and High Performance

A basic premise of this book is that high performance is a necessity for organizational success. The "anchor" initiative necessary to achieve a high-performing organization is empowerment. In other words, high performance is not possible without simultaneously creating an empowered organization. The reason empowerment is the anchor initiative is because it is the foundation upon which all of the high-involvement initiatives are based when put into practice. In this sense, a high-performance organization is one which has successfully integrated and institutionalized teamwork; quality; work process redesign (reengineering); environment, safety, and health (ES&H); customer focus; diversity; and empowerment. An illustration of this definition is shown as Figure 2. These are all high-involvement initiatives that require personally empowered employees.

A high-performance organization is:

1) Customer focused

2) Highly empowered — individually and collectively

3) Continuously improving

4) Receptive to change

5) Diverse

6) Knowledge-based

7) Global (decentralized)

Each of these seven characteristics will be briefly woven together in the following discussion.

The four key elements of a *customer-focused* organization have been previously discussed — they are quality, customization, speed, and service. We suggest that these are also the crucial requirements for surviving, as a business, during the remainder of the 1990s. In order to operate consistent with these four elements, an organization requires highly competent employees who have the freedom to perform their responsibilities with the least amount of management and direction — *highly empowered employees*. Solutions, in large part, will have to originate with those closest to the problems. Employee-customer partnerships are encouraged

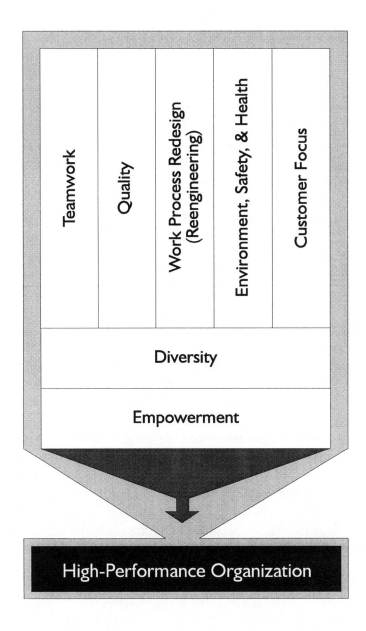

Figure 2.   The integrated initiatives of a high-performance organization

wherever practical and/or sensible. Such a partnership serves as a basis for the *continuous improvement* of products, goods, and services from the established employee-customer feedback relationship.

A result of continuously changing customer demands is that new products and the processes necessary to produce them are changing almost monthly and, in some cases, daily. We live and work in a period where *change* is so rapid and unpredictable that we have to learn to become comfortable with chaos and ambiguity. That is, we must be simultaneously receptive and responsive to change, and then learn to anticipate it by being on the leading edge of change. A profound element of recent change is the recognition of the value of *diversity*, particularly since the world's work force and customer base are diverse.

Diversity-thinking provides the opportunity for higher quality decision making, problem solving, innovation, and creativity as compared to homogeneous thinking. Thus, diversity has the potential to be a significant competitive advantage if aggressively utilized. In the present *knowledge-based* era, competitive advantage can be maintained only where there are continuously learning knowledge workers. The final characteristic is the recognition that corporations compete in a borderless *global economy*. Customers can acquire any product or service, of the highest quality, from anywhere in the world. Taken together as an integrated way of functioning, these seven characteristics define a high-performance organization.

Consider how many of these characteristics are already part of your organization's way of doing business. If you recognize very few in practice, begin to consider what you can personally do to light a fire. Although challenging, it may not be as difficult as you think.

♦ Empowerment Requires Fundamental Change

The reason empowerment is so challenging is that we must not only change the way we organize and perform work, but we must also *fundamentally change* our traditional beliefs, attitudes, and assumptions about work. Such fundamental change is more accurately defined as personal and organizational transformation.

Empowerment requires transformation of our fundamental beliefs about:

1) Personal responsibility and accountability

2) Performance

3) Self-motivated continuous learning

4) Value-added employment

5) Self-management

6) Teamwork

7) Change

8) Leadership

Here is how our attitudes will have to change in order for empowerment to work:

1) **Personal Responsibility and Accountability** — In order for expanded responsible delegation to occur, employees will have to assume greater charge of their work tasks. They will have to plan with greater care and knowledge, anticipate pitfalls, and design solutions in advance. In the end, personal accountability means

ownership of the results — successful and unsuccessful — without any reasons or excuses. This attitude provides the basis for new learning when the results are unsuccessful.

2) **Performance** — Empowerment will force us to encounter and move beyond self-imposed limitations about our capabilities to perform. The greatest challenge we face in expanding our performance is not in learning new skills, but in changing our strongly held *beliefs* about what we should or should not be required to do in this new high-involvement environment. What we will have to learn and accept is that we should change in whatever way necessary (within moral and ethical bounds) to exceed our customers' expectations — both internal and external.

3) **Self-Motivated Continuous Learning** — In the present knowledge-based era, continuous learning is a necessity. Without continuous learning, an employee jeopardizes her or his value to an organization. In high-involvement organizations, greater personal responsibility means the individual is self-motivated to acquire new learning by being in constant contact with the continuously changing needs of customers.

4) **Value-Added Employment** — This requirement principally involves a shift in mindset from entitlement to believing that "my employment is based upon the continuing value I bring to internal or external customers. In essence, I do not work for a company, I work for a customer. I have the highest probability for secure employment when I exceed my identified customer's expectations. This mode of thinking allows me to accurately define value-added work."

5) **Self-Management** — A natural consequence of expanded delegation with less oversight is the necessity for each employee to assume management responsibilities previously performed by his or her manager. It is important to realize that management does not disappear; it is simply passed on to the employee. A crucial aspect of this new responsibility is the ability to organize and prioritize one's work independently. In the initial stages, coaching and mentoring may be necessary.

6) **Teamwork** — The shift from focus on self to group is probably the most difficult of all for many Western-oriented individuals — those primarily motivated by individual self-interest. It involves an expanded perspective to authentically value and practice teamwork. It requires the realization that business competitiveness and success will be a balance of synergistic group interdependence *and* the full expression of individual excellence.

7) **Change** — This element principally involves adopting a mindset that rapid change is a way of life. What appears to be chaos and confusion, because so many things are happening simultaneously, is the new norm. It is the acceptance of a mindset that an employee's job is a continuously changing function of what internal and external customers want and need. This change is created by unpredictable events referred to as chaos. The key here is to relinquish the necessity for personal control or security.

8) **Leadership** — Empowering leadership involves the continual process of creating expanded competence and giving away responsibility. It is a shift from an individually led mindset to a participative leadership mindset. This means that leadership exists at every level of

an organization. The focus is on establishing a high standard of excellence and inspiring employees to self-enroll in committing to achieve that level of performance.

Empowerment in Action

A crucial requirement for the success of empowerment is that individual employees fulfill delegated authority through a strong sense of self-accountability. An outstanding example of an organization which makes this fundamental assumption of all of its employees is W. L. Gore and Associates, Inc. in Flagstaff, Arizona. This corporation assumes that if you treat people as responsible adults, they will respond as such in turn. This is one of the most important principles upon which this organization has been based since its founding in the late 1950s.

As an example, when a new technical employee joins Gore, she or he is encouraged to discuss projects with a number of working groups in order to decide how she or he might bring the greatest value to the organization, rather than have the organization make an outright job assignment. In this way the organization fosters employee ownership and commitment to its goals. This obvious yet powerful assumption is the basis for the high degree of empowerment and success their employees experience individually and as a corporation. This is an example of an organization which has chosen to operate at the far right side of Figure 1. Every organization should make a similar choice based upon its unique work force and customer requirements.

Simultaneous with this focus on the individual is an interdependent network of individuals and organizational units that *require* each other's contribution for success. For example, in a consulting firm an individual in Research and Development may come up with a brilliant idea for a sales presentation. By the time it is delivered to a client audience, however, it has involved computer (and graphic) specialists, sales and marketing personnel, scheduling, materials disbursement, sales presentation arrangements, and finally the individual who makes the presentation. Without the cooperation and self-accountability of each of these units, the delivery of that presentation to a client audience would lack total quality service in some way. Even though the individual making the presentation might appear to be the star, each individual and group involved in that process are equally stars. In an empowered organization, they are genuinely valued and acknowledged as such.

Having established an understanding of empowerment and its fundamental role in creating a high-performance organization, we can now proceed to discuss the principles upon which empowerment is based.

Chapter 3. **Principles of Empowerment**

♦ Introduction

In this chapter we outline the principles of empowerment. These principles define the structure, guidelines, and functions managers need in order to effectively implement an empowerment initiative. Principles provide the guidelines for desired and undesired behaviors. They make a statement to employees and the public as to what an organization stands for. Principles not only serve as guidelines, but also as the basis for learning experiences when breakdowns or difficulties occur.

In a performance review, an employee was rated poorly in interpersonal relationships. He learned that more than 50 percent of the people in the organization regarded their relationship with him as poor. In a conversation with his manager, he was informed that it was doubtful that he could be productive with such incompatibilities. Furthermore, he was strongly urged to immediately enroll in the appropriate in-house training in order to ensure continued employment. His manager also informed him that personal growth was a way of life in their organization and was one of the organization's most important principles. Therefore, his interpersonal difficulty was not only about remedying a situation, but also about creating an understanding that personal growth was an ongoing process. The point is, the performance review provided an opportunity to not only solve a problem involving interpersonal relationships, but to teach a principle.

♦ Principles of Empowerment

Implementing principles of empowerment can be challenging because it involves a radical shift from our traditional way of operating. The following principles include the most important elements for creating an empowered organization:

1) *People are an organization's most valuable resource.*

   The founding principle of empowerment is that people are more important than management systems. The essence of this principle is that the manner in which a management system operates is determined by the people who comprise the organization. It assumes that people are not expendable units because they bring differences which may force the system of operation to change. Although projects may come and go, the most vital recyclable resource, which is utilized over and over again, is people. For this reason, it is necessary to preserve the mental, physical, emotional, and even the spiritual well-being of employees. In the present progression from the information era to the knowledge-based era, the development, utilization, and retention of creative and innovative employees will determine the survival of an organization.

2) *High-involvement is maximized.*

   High-involvement is based upon the assumption that the more employees are involved in designing and controlling their work functions, the more productively and efficiently the organization will operate. The basis of this assumption is that structured management systems severely limit the performance capacities of employees. For high-involvement to work, employees must assume responsibility and accountability for understanding and ensuring the successful production of a whole aspect of work. Individually and collectively, employees must have a high degree of self-discipline and self-management in order to operate with the least amount of oversight or management. The crucial fact to understand is that in today's hyperaccelerated world, high-involvement is inevitable.

3) *Teamwork is valued and rewarded.*

Teamwork has three major advantages: 1) A whole aspect of a product or service which involves several or many parts (steps) can be performed simultaneously; 2) teams provide the opportunity for synergism which is not possible for an individual working alone; and 3) team functioning, over a sustained period, preserves the overall health and well-being of employees. Empowered teams have two vital elements: 1) the full expression of individual excellence; and 2) the necessity (or preference) for interdependence in order to achieve the team goal. Teamwork is essential for the success of empowerment since so few products and services can be delivered today by the efforts of a single employee. When this principle is applied to an organization, the organization is viewed as a network of interdependent centers of excellence. The commitment to team projects must be balanced with commitment to the overall success of the organization.

4) *Personal and professional growth are continuous.*

Personal growth and professional development are *a way of life in empowered organizations*. Since empowerment is a *dynamic process* rather than a specific goal to be reached, there is the sequential cycle of self-motivated goal setting and achievement, which continually drives the enhanced capability of employees (page 4). High-involvement necessitates people-oriented skills, hence the corresponding necessity for continual personal growth. The most severe limitation to performance in high-involvement organizations is employees' reluctance to proactively accept the process of personal growth. This principle also makes a job interesting, fun, and creative because of the necessity for continuous improvement.

5) *Responsibility and accountability are maximized.*

Empowerment is based upon maximizing individual and collective responsibility and accountability. This means a predisposed mindset of total responsibility for projects or tasks which are delegated. Such a mindset has the potential for not only meeting but exceeding customer or client expectations. Without a critical fraction of highly responsible and accountable employees, empowerment is not possible. The more difficult of these two requirements is holding self and others accountable. Accountability is probably *the* limiting factor in determining the extent to which high-involvement is possible.

6) *Self-determination, self-motivation, and self-management are expected.*

An inherent assumption of empowerment is that most, if not all, employees have the talent and capability to perform their jobs and responsibilities with the least amount of direction. The limitation in fully living up to their capability is commonly a mindset which compromises self-determination in difficult situations. Where the talent or capability is lacking, principle (4) above applies. An additional assumption is that the incentive to meet (and possibly exceed) job expectations comes from within an individual. Given principles (4) and (5) above and a clear organizational support system, employees are expected to be self-driven in terms of determination, motivation, and management.

7) *Expanded delegation is a continual process.*

It is vitally important to understand that the act of delegation is not empowerment. The procedure for *implementing* empowerment is delegation of responsibility within clearly defined guidelines. Empowerment ultimately depends most on an individual's ability to perform the expanded responsibility which has been delegated. A requirement of expanded delegation is ensuring that an individual or a team is maximally prepared to accept the expanded responsibility. A central issue to the success of empowerment is giving up control. This act requires trust and the willingness to share information, knowledge, and power. The question a manager constantly asks himself or herself in an empowering environment is, "How do I mentor and coach what I do, and give it away?" This means that mentoring and coaching become critical management skills in support of delegation. Teams provide a natural process for mentoring and coaching relationships.

8) *Hierarchy is minimized.*

A natural consequence of extensive delegation is the systematic reduction of hierarchy. Hierarchical organizational structures discourage empowerment by supporting a line-of-authority system and discouraging cross-functional teams. Cross-functional teams focus on clients or customers, products, goods, or services. This principle, in an indirect way, means that influence and authority are based on *demonstrated* competence, performance, and an ability to manage oneself, rather than solely on position power. In today's fast-paced business environment, hierarchical structures or systems of operation are simply too cumbersome and slow to respond to market demands.

9) *Organizational leadership and support are necessary to drive and sustain empowerment.*

Empowerment cannot exist without a clear commitment from organizational leadership. Leadership must communicate the necessity or desirability for empowerment and link it to the organization's opportunity for greater success. The support system involves the systematic change in processes, procedures, structures, and a redesign in the way work is done, e.g., greater emphasis on teamwork. The simplest way to express this principle is that leadership and management must *live* the empowerment vision and *model* the values by putting into visible practice what is preached. For empowerment to take hold, leaders must be living examples of the principles discussed in this chapter.

These principles provide the context within which empowerment is practiced. Some principles are more easily applied than others, depending on the nature of the organization and its traditional culture. For example, the way empowerment is practiced in Japan or Mexico may be radically different from the United States, simply because of significant cultural differences. In Japan, preserving face may have a profound effect on the way holding others accountable is done as compared to the United States where the process may be more or less confrontational. In Mexico, a respected elder may be more influential in critical business decisions than someone younger and less experienced. In the United States, by contrast, age actually may be viewed as a liability in important business decisions. Whatever the unique processes or customs of a culture, empowerment is a performance-based system of management where vital principles cannot be compromised.

We suggest that as you begin implementation, you take the path of least resistance, such as implementing and rewarding teamwork. Then gradually implementing the more challenging principles, such as the reduction of hierarchy and the delegation of greater authority. The basis for granting greater authority is the subject of the next chapter. It establishes the foundation upon which empowerment is based.

Chapter 4. **Foundation of Empowerment**

♦ Introduction

This is probably the most important chapter in this book. It establishes the foundation upon which empowerment is based. This foundation involves an experiential understanding and acceptance of three important concepts: *personal responsibility*, *personal accountability*, and *personal empowerment*. We will show that ability and skills are necessary but not sufficient for high performance. These competencies must be driven by personality characteristics which are derived from a mindset of total responsibility for one's life. We conclude the chapter with a set of guidelines for continually expanding one's professional performance.

♦ Personal Responsibility

Personal responsibility is the willingness to view yourself as the *principal source* of the results and circumstances which occur in your life, both individually and collectively with others in the workplace.

This is a challenging requirement. However, it is based upon the experience of life as it exists, not upon the assumption that life should be fair. The emphasis in this definition is on creating a mindset which focuses power in the individual. It minimizes the focus on circumstances which relegate us to a victim role — even in situations which are unfair or unreasonable. In fact, we are tested most in these types of situations. The major barriers that often immobilize us are our own self-limiting beliefs about ourselves or the external environment. These beliefs are based upon how we feel the world should be as compared to how it is.

To make this point, I (BG) would like to share my space ship story. I imagine myself to be from another reality called LaCornia. I arrive on earth from a space ship and assume the identity of a black American from the South. Fortunately, I have no memory of slavery, no realization I am a minority (and therefore not seeking to become equal), and no expectation (or realization) of what is fair or unfair by earth's rules. By the way, I have also not read the book *The Bell Curve*. I examine my unique circumstances and the challenges (not barriers) I face and set a strategy to achieve my goals. Since I also don't understand win/lose, it is immaterial whether I succeed or not, because participating all out gives me the greatest satisfaction of being human — living up to my full potential.

This is the point. What I discovered from this story was that the greatest difference between my space self and my real self was the battle occurring in my head. My space self focused totally on what he wanted to accomplish, without the expectation of fairness. In fact, he viewed the never-ending array of barriers as challenges to sharpen his skills and competencies, while my real self saw them as reasons to become frustrated and finally give up. Now I think I understand the expression, "It's not whether you win or lose; it's how you play the game!"

This story is obviously fiction and probably unrealistic. However, it does point out that there is an alternative approach to life when circumstances appear to be unfair. The hook is that it requires us to accept responsibility for situations we find ourselves in when we believe others are the cause. This hook is very, very difficult to accept, but embracing it can be extremely powerful in terms of how we approach life!

With this mindset, we can focus on producing results in the most proactive manner, without the excess expenditure of time, work, or energy. We don't fool ourselves into believing that unfairness does not exist, but we simply choose to spend as little time as possible bemoaning that situation. So taking responsibility for our life is accepting what we have, no matter how it got there!

Think about it a minute. We are only as powerful in life as we are responsible. This statement plays out everywhere. In the workplace we are most effective in managing others in the areas which we have personally claimed responsibility for ourselves. In a like manner, we are least effective in those areas for which we have been marginally responsible.

In the above definition of personal responsibility, *principal source* can be as great or as little as you choose. There is no restriction as to how responsible you believe you are for the results which occur in your life. You can just as easily believe you are 90 percent responsible as you can believe you are 50 percent responsible. However, the results consistently produced over time by each of these mindsets are worlds apart. The 90 percent individual accomplishes most, if not all, of the goals he or she establishes, whereas the 50 percent individual, in general, has a constant array of reasons and excuses why he or she did not succeed. Typically, these reasons and excuses are based upon how the world or people should change in order for that individual to be successful. If it is one lesson we eventually learn, it is that people have absolutely no interest in changing one iota to accommodate us! So what's the message? There is no help coming! Get on with your life!

♦ Personal Accountability

Personal accountability is the willingness to *claim ownership* for the results which are produced as a consequence of your involvement, both individually and collectively, with others in the workplace.

The key word in this definition is *ownership*. If we assume ownership for whatever occurs, we can take charge of initiating the appropriate action. If we abdicate ownership, then we feel powerless to take action. Therefore, outside assistance is necessary to initiate positive change in our behalf. Furthermore, the extent to which managers and employees can proactively hold others accountable is directly proportional to the extent to which they assume personal responsibility. Thus, responsibility and accountability are complementary sides of the same coin. Through ownership of the difficulties as well as the successes in the workplace, the truly successful manager or employee recognizes the opportunity for feedback, growth, and the acquisition of new skills in the areas where deficiencies exist.

Accountability sounds very similar to "you reap what you sow." The problem arises when we do not consciously know what we sowed but we reaped the consequences anyway. This result alone would lead us to live our lives as if everything that happened to us was in some way planned by us. To understand this point of view, we would like to share with you A Tale of Woe.

A Tale of Woe

Stan entered into a signed agreement with another business to produce a new breakthrough product in information technology. Much of the agreement involved good faith on both their parts. That is, they had expectations of each other regarding their joint effort in producing the product as well as selling the product once it was completed. They agreed to split the profits equally from joint or separate efforts. The production was very successful. However, the sales direction of the other business changed and the jointly produced product was no longer a high priority. In fact, there were no specific plans for a sales strategy or a specific goal of unit sales. Stan had very specific plans and had borrowed a large sum of money to promote the product.

The Hitch: Stan wants to change the equal split and allow each partner to sell the product separately and to earn separate profits. The other business wants the agreement to remain as is. Stan refuses.

- Did Stan sow the seeds of the impasse? Definitely.
- Is Stan accountable for the impasse? Yes.
- Could the impasse have been avoided? Probably not.
- Why? Good faith only works when the individuals involved have overlapping values and practice them with high integrity.

The Conclusion: Their value systems are different. The value system of the other business says, "Things change, but a signed agreement is a signed agreement." Stan's value system says, "When things change, the signed agreement should change."

The Resolution: Resort to the legal system. Again!

The Point: Accountability goes beyond ethics, values, signed agreements, etc. Accountability simply means that if it happened in your life, you own it! It's almost like accountability is a higher law operating above all the reasons, explanations, excuses, and articulate arguments!

The Completion: Was the other business also accountable? Absolutely! 100 percent.

Guillory and Galindo

The Responsibility Scale

In order to acquire a quantitative sense of these concepts, we have developed a responsibility scale, shown as Figure 3. This scale is based upon a very important assumption: *Every individual has available 100 percent personal responsibility for the events which occur in his or her life, as a theoretical limit.* The scale shown as Figure 3a is representative of an individual who assumes he or she is, on average, 50 percent personally responsible and therefore 50 percent personally accountable. *If* the assumption of 100 percent *availability* is valid, this individual abdicates 50 percent responsibility and he or she feels victimized and disempowered to influence those events.

The illustration shown as Figure 3b is for an individual who assumes 70 percent personal responsibility, on average, for the events which occur in her or his life. We can see how the victim-disempowered area is diminished relative to the responsible-accountable area. Figure 3c illustrates an individual whose predisposed assumption of personal responsibility is 90 percent. This mindset is indicative of an individual who achieves, on average, most of his or her established goals in life. The top scale in this figure has the phrase *Personal Empowerment.* Thus, we can begin to understand that the most important requirement for personal empowerment is the assumption of a high degree of personal responsibility and accountability. In essence, there is no such thing as a highly empowered individual who does not also claim a high degree of personal responsibility and accountability. The relationship between these three vitally important concepts is summarized by the following statement: *An individual is personally empowered only to the extent he or she assumes a predisposed mindset of personal responsibility and accountability.*

The Responsibility Scale

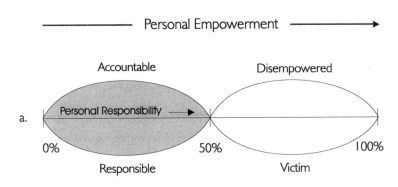

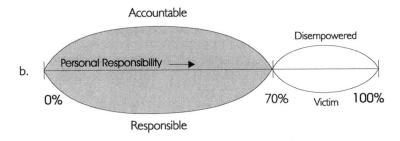

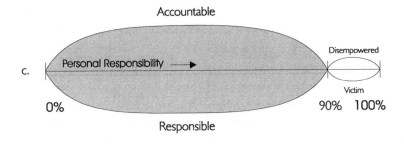

Figure 3.   Personal responsibility and accountability represented on a 0 to 100 percent scale. A high level of personal empowerment corresponds to a high level of personal responsibility and accountability.

Guillory and Galindo

The following story illustrates how these concepts can transform an employee's mindset when learned as an experiential process.

> The announcement of an empowerment initiative in Julio's organization brought great excitement. Based on their understanding of it, many employees felt it was long overdue. For too long, managers who were too far removed from the actual work had controlled how work was organized. Julio hoped that this would mean that the dictator-like manager over his department would be ousted or get the message and leave.
>
> To his surprise, the first training Julio was offered had to do with becoming a personally empowered, self-motivated, continuously learning employee! "As usual, they want more out of me," Julio thought. "When are they going to do something about these managers!" As the training progressed, he realized that management control wasn't necessarily the problem. Through realistic case studies he learned that no matter what, he was responsible and accountable for the results he produced. It was hard to understand at first.
>
> Over time, the scapegoats for lack of individual production began falling away and the organization was slowly putting in a support system for the new learning. His manager is still over the department and has become much more of a resource than a barrier. Julio realized his manager was not the only one who underwent new learning.

This story shows that organizational transformation begins with each individual employee realizing his or her own responsibility to change. This realization creates ownership of the change initiative. This individual can now become a credible change agent who influences this change in others. As this type of process occurs with greater frequency, an organization eventually achieves the critical mass necessary to transform the organizational culture.

48

◆ Personal Empowerment

Personal empowerment is an *internally-derived* capacity to perform at or above an established level of expectation. It is expanded by going beyond both self-imposed and external limitations through continuous learning.

Personal empowerment is the process of invalidating self-imposed beliefs *and* organizational barriers which serve to limit exceptional performance. If the ability to perform comes from within, it means that no one can personally empower someone else with the ability to perform. It also means that the act of delegation is not empowerment, but *is* a vitally important mode of operation in the achievement of an empowered organization.

For example, an employee may strongly believe that he or she should not have to compete on an uneven playing field. If that belief serves to limit his or her performance, then it is self-imposed, regardless of the fact that the playing field may, in fact, be uneven. The question is, "What do I do now with the circumstances that presently exist, while the organization and certain key individuals are working to 'level the playing field?' " Although this is a question that each individual has to answer for himself or herself, an empowering suggestion would be to use every opportunity to further personal and professional growth, confident in the fact that you are preparing yourself for your personal goal. The achievement of your goal may be with your present organization or with another that is more receptive to your advancement and success.

In a like manner, another employee may feel victimized and stymied by certain actions on the part of the organization to create a level playing field. This is an example of an apparent external limitation for that individual. Sometimes such actions are referred to as reverse discrimination. The recommendation to an empowered individual is to accept the fact that real, level competition from traditionally underutilized segments of the organization will be the way of the future. A new element in the promotion and advancement process will be a committed effort that *no one* will be denied advancement because of race, color, sex, religion, sexual orientation, national origin, etc., *and* that concrete steps in assessment and planning will be taken to ensure this commitment. When this reality is nonreactively accepted, it will be realized that such a commitment benefits *everyone* in the long run. The employee is challenged to take this new reality into consideration as he or she plans a career strategy, rather than focusing on the unfairness of the situation.

This type of situation is illustrated by the following example of "Eugene's World."

Eugene's world was changing faster than he could cope. Last month it was some diversity thing they all had to go to and tomorrow the right-sizing plan would be announced. He had been in line for a much-awaited promotion and now the chances seemed minimal that it would come through. Why wasn't Mark rattled? Nothing seemed to faze him. He even walked off right in the middle of a complaint session by a group of employees, and he had every right to be angry. A woman got the supervisor's job that should have been his! When Eugene had a chance to talk things over with Mark, the response surprised him. "It's a new world; we have to pay attention and prepare. Janet deserved the job and I, for one, plan to help make her successful. Anything less and I'd be hurting my own future opportunities. The diversity initiative makes sense. I'll plan a new strategy for my success and be ready for whatever comes. Just because I can't control what's happening in our work environment doesn't mean I'm not responsible for my own success." Eugene walked away thinking "Maybe he understands something I don't."

The more proactive agents of change there are to assist others into the new reality, the more constructive the process will be. In the short run, what might appear to be inequities will in most cases turn out to be in everyone's best interest. Competent, high-performing people are rarely, if ever, not rewarded in a timely manner.

Understanding personal empowerment and how it becomes a learned skill is crucial to behaving in an empowered way or implementing management by empowerment. It is equally important to understand that someone cannot personally empower someone else; empowerment comes from within. However, through the establishment of a relationship based upon *mutual respect, trust,* and *equality,* it becomes possible to mentor or coach the proactive empowerment of an employee, a team member, or a co-worker.

♦ The Empowered Individual

In the discussion above, we established that the extent to which an individual is personally empowered is measured by her or his demonstrated ability to perform. Therefore, personality characteristics (i.e., self-motivation) drive natural and learned competencies to generate professional performance, as shown in Figure 4. Personality characteristics are primarily an indication of an individual's mindset. In an overall sense, it characterizes the extent to which an individual is personally driven, *from within,* to succeed in spite of situations or circumstances. Most successful people believe that this component is more important than natural and learned competencies. That is, without the drive to succeed, natural and learned competencies will be only marginally used.

The Empowered Individual

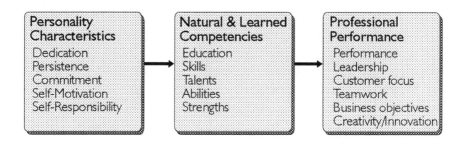

Figure 4.   Personality characteristics drive natural and learned competencies, which result in an individual's measurable performance.

Education and skills are also vitally important in determining the performance of an individual. The greater the knowledge and skills, the more *potentially* exceptional the individual's performance. Merely having a degree from a prestigious academic institution (even with high grades) does not ensure a highly productive employee over the course of a career. In a like manner, an individual from a lesser-known institution (with high grades) may actually perform in an exceptional manner over the course of a career; particularly if traditional systemic barriers of elitism are removed and *all* employees are encouraged to perform to the full extent of their inherent abilities.

Avon has developed an excellent Performance Development Process (PDP) instrument. In evaluating an associate's professional performance, job objectives:

- are linked to the business plan/goals;
- are both challenging and achievable;

- have time targets;
- are measurable in some way; and
- are agreed upon by both the associate and manager.

Expanding Your Personal Empowerment

The following set of guidelines is designed to assist you in systematically and proactively expanding your personal empowerment:

1) *Assess your present level of personal empowerment.*

   Honestly evaluate your present level of personal and professional mastery of your job by soliciting input from a broad spectrum of sources.

2) *Determine whether your performance falls below, meets, or exceeds customer expectations.*

   Assess the quality of your performance through the eyes of your internal and external customers.

3) *If your performance is below expectations, assess your level of commitment.*

   If your performance is below expectations and you are sufficiently skilled for your present job, seriously re-examine whether you are committed to meeting the expectations of your present job. If not, make plans for doing something else.

4) *If committed, determine the new skills you require.*

   If you feel you are committed to meeting the expectations of your present job, write in detail the new personal and/or professional skills you require based upon expanded responsibility and accountability.

5) *Acquire a mentor/coach to hold you accountable.*

   Acquire a mentor or a coach to assist you and hold you accountable to your commitment, based upon the results you produce.

6) *Overcome your self-limitations.*

   When you encounter a barrier, have your mentor facilitate you in overcoming it. Remember, it is ultimately *your* responsibility to take charge of invalidating your self-limiting belief(s) by designing and performing noncomfort-zone actions.

7) *If committed to expanded empowerment, define a new challenging area of activity.*

   If you meet or exceed your present job expectations, describe a project or an area of activity you would enjoy which involves significantly expanded responsibility in terms of the acquisition of new personal and/or professional skills.

8) *Proceed and apply steps (5) and (6) where difficulties occur.*

   Begin the project, utilizing and/or learning proven professional methods and knowledge. If difficulties or problems occur, apply steps (5) and (6) above.

◆ Summary of Important Empowerment Concepts

For employees:

1) No one can *personally empower* you with the ability to perform.

2) You can be empowered with decision-making and problem-solving authority — this is delegation.

3) The process of personal empowerment can be *facilitated* by a manager or co-worker through coaching and mentoring.

4) The process of empowerment is the basis for personal and professional development.

5) Personal empowerment is your responsibility, whether or not the organization provides a supportive environment.

For managers:

1) You cannot *personally empower* anyone with the ability to perform.

2) You can empower others with decision-making and problem-solving authority — this is delegation.

3) You can facilitate or coach the personal empowerment of a co-worker.

4) You cannot coach the *proactive* empowerment of a co-worker if you do not respect and accept her or him as fully equal and capable.

5) You cannot facilitate in others what you have not learned about yourself.

6) Employees need to be managed to the extent they are not personally empowered through continuous learning.

Guillory and Galindo

In the next chapter we discuss processes for having personal responsibility, accountability, and empowerment become functional skills in the workplace.

Chapter 5. Learning Fundamental Empowerment Skills

♦ Introduction

We indicated at the beginning of the previous chapter that implementing empowerment requires an experiential understanding and acceptance of personal responsibility, accountability, and empowerment. The first exercise in this chapter is designed to have you *experience* what we really mean by the definitions we proposed in the previous chapter. The second exercise provides a procedure for applying these concepts to "stretch" work projects. As this procedure is used repeatedly, these three concepts will become functional skills that you use without conscious thinking.

♦ The Network Is Down — An Empowerment Exercise

The primary objective of this exercise is to internalize the meaning of the terms *personal responsibility, accountability,* and *empowerment.* It can be done alone or, preferably, with a group of not more than six (6) participants. The exercise begins with each participant declaring to what extent, on a 0 percent to 100 percent scale, she or he believes the following quote:

> *Individuals carry their success or their*
> *failure with them . . . it does not*
> *depend on outside conditions . . .*

Ralph Waldo Trine

Example: *"I believe 70 percent of my success depends on me and 30 percent on outside conditions."*

Participant's answer: _____%

Instructions:

1) Read the story on the following page (page 59).

2) Complete the True/False quiz alone (page 60).

3) Through discussion, reach group consensus[†] regarding each of the True/False statements within your group. The discussion time is limited to one hour.

4) Select someone in the group to record your group rationale for each True/False group answer (page 61).

[†] **Group consensus** is the collective agreement of the group which includes the minority opinion as an integrated part of the group decision.

THE NETWORK IS DOWN!

The leadership of an Information Management Corporation decides to aggressively incorporate an Empowerment Initiative throughout the organization to complement their ongoing quality program. Managers are asked to delegate more authority to employees and to create teams across divisions. One of the more enterprising teams designs an interdivisional communications network system. The team insists on working independently, with little or no input from management. The network system also bypasses most of the previous decision-making authority of the team members' direct managers. During the design phase, team members complain of unnecessary bureaucracy and a lack of critical and timely information flow from management. The direct managers, who previously had strict guidelines for information dissemination, have no new guidelines from the senior leadership on what information can be distributed. When the new system is initially made operational, breakdown occurs. After the system is restored and functioning for three months, it is evaluated to be less efficient and less cost-effective than the previous communications system. The senior leadership promises to make a decision regarding the continuation of the team project after studying the evaluation.

Guillory and Galindo

Based on the story on the previous page, individually circle the following choices as True (T) or False (F).

1) The interdivisional team members were each personally responsible for the system breakdown.   T   F

2) The direct managers were responsible for ensuring the success of the interdivisional team.   T   F

3) To some degree, management control of employees is necessary.   T   F

4) Supervision is unnecessary for an employee who feels he or she is personally empowered.   T   F

5) The direct managers were responsible and accountable for providing the necessary information to the team.   T   F

6) The senior leadership was not committed to the empowerment initiative.   T   F

7) The direct managers were accountable for the system breakdown irrespective of whether or not their input was included.   T   F

8) The senior leadership was 100 percent responsible and 100 percent accountable for the entire situation.   T   F

THE NETWORK IS DOWN!

A Group Decision-Making Exercise

After discussing your individual choices on the previous page, please circle your group's T/F choice and record a brief statement of the rationale of your group in reaching consensus.

1) T   F :

2) T   F :

3) T   F :

4) T   F :

5) T   F :

6) T   F :

7) T   F :

8) T   F :

Guillory and Galindo

Each True/False statement in the exercise on page 60 was designed to illustrate an operational principle of empowerment. If we base our criteria for each True or False answer on the opportunity for professional development, teamwork, and organizational productivity, the following answers and operational principles become important for empowered performance. Your team can compare its True/False answers with the answers we have suggested below.

THE NETWORK IS DOWN!

Operational Principles for Empowerment

1) **True** Principle: Each team member is simultaneously 100 percent responsible for his or her unique participation and 100 percent responsible for the results produced by the team. This principle establishes a truly unique paradigm of performance and achievement.

2) **True** Principle: Managers are individually responsible for whatever occurs in their domain of authority irrespective of the circumstances.

3) **False** Principle: Management control of *employees* stifles empowerment and is impractical. However, management control of *processes* is important in the initial stages of implementing empowerment when employees are still learning the process.

4) **False** Principle: "*Feeling* empowered is the Grand Canyon away from *being* empowered."

5) **True** Principle: Direct managers are responsible and accountable for supporting the success of a team under their supervision.

6) **True** Principle: Commitment is *confirmed* when the inevitable difficulty of greatest challenge is successfully overcome.

7) **True** Principle: Managers are 100 percent accountable for breakdowns just as they are accountable for successes.

8) **True** Principle: "The buck stops here!" — Harry S. Truman.

The objective of these suggested answers and principles is not only to clearly understand what is meant by the definitions of personal responsibility, accountability, and empowerment on pages 41, 43, and 49, but to create a new paradigm of thinking. This paradigm has the power to place an organization in a truly unique class in terms of high employee involvement. The widespread adoption of this organizational mindset is a requirement for becoming a high-performance organization as illustrated by the diagram on page 25.

Summary of important empowerment principles raised in this case study:

1) Incorporating empowerment requires much more than a directive from the senior leadership, i.e., an empowerment support system.

2) The establishment of basic principles and definitions of empowerment organization-wide is necessary for the successful implementation of empowerment.

3) Middle managers (with vast experience, knowledge, and skills) are crucial to the success of empowerment.

4) The change process requires expanded interpersonal and negotiation skills to have a smooth transition.

5) Instituting a new culture and system will almost invariably be less efficient and less productive in the short run, particularly where education and training are not provided.

6) Commitment is typically measured by how decisively leadership responds when a difficulty or crisis occurs.

When the performance of a team is limited or severely hampered because of resistance to necessary and inevitable change, it is difficult, if not impossible, to implement organizational empowerment.

If you performed this exercise as a team, you were provided the opportunity to experience interpersonal team dynamics in attempting to reach consensus. The next section provides an opportunity to discuss and gain value from your team's experience.

♦ Interpersonal Team Skills

One of the reasons for instructing the team to reach consensus (as we defined it) is that it is rarely achievable in a one-hour time frame. Team members often resort to what they most commonly do in pressured situations in order to achieve agreement. The result is typically a vote. Voting is an example of *individualism* in which the majority carries. This is *not* consensus as defined on page 58. Consensus requires more give-and-take, and seeing the points of view of others through their eyes. The result is that most team members acquire a different perspective by the end of the discussion, as compared to where they started.

Consensus, in a Japanese way of operating, is probably not the best way for U.S. Americans to operate. This form of consensus is culturally based. It provides the opportunity for each person to fully express their point of view in an uninterrupted manner. There is much deliberation, discussion, and time for personal processing before reaching a consensus. U.S. Americans, however, tend to be more fact-based in the decision-making process and less intuitive. The assumption is that if the facts are logically put together, the conclusion (and hence the decision) is obvious. Your team may have experienced these two different approaches in the exercise. Perhaps somewhere between the two is optimal for team consensus. We suggest "collaborative agreement."[2] The definitions of these two words capture the essence of what we mean:

- Collaborative — to work jointly with others

- Agreement — harmony of opinion or action; mutual understanding

Adopting this approach can result in the efficient use of time while simultaneously maximizing input and team alignment.

Since constructive interpersonal behavior is important for effective team operation, your group might discuss what each of you discovered about your own behavior in that exercise. Your team's discussion might address the following three points:

1) What did you learn most about yourself in attempting to reach group consensus?

2) How receptive were you to opinions from others that were different from your own?

3) As an option, your team members might give feedback to each other based on their experiences of each other's behaviors.

Use the list of interpersonal team skills described below as a guideline for your discussion.

1) **Self-Observation** — the examination of your feelings, emotions, and behaviors in relating to others who are different and think differently. The following behaviors indicate a discomfort with such differences:

   - dominating a discussion
   - being inwardly (or outwardly) angry
   - cutting others off
   - not being open and receptive to differences
   - defensiveness

2) **Open Communication** — the *experience* of being free to honestly express opinions different from others. The following behaviors indicate open communication:

   - allowing complete explanations
   - expressing yourself fully even when there is a reaction
   - encouraging others not to interrupt
   - being concise, brief, and to the point

3) **Suspension of Assumptions** — the willingness to set aside beliefs about others and what they have to say. The following behaviors indicate suspension of assumptions:

   - realize that assumptions are rarely accurate
   - avoid making unsupported charges

- create dialogue around the issue which is most troubling

4) **Dialogue** — to be totally open to another's point of view in a discussion. The following behaviors indicate dialogue:

   - listen to your own self-talk
   - attempt to set the self-talk aside
   - put yourself in another's shoes
   - express your point of view in a convincing manner

Finally, each of your team members might discuss how she or he plans to use the insights from this exercise to behave differently in the future.

♦ Foundation of Empowerment — An Exercise

We have suggested that personal responsibility, accountability, and empowerment are the foundation upon which high-involvement is based. Upon closer examination, these concepts are also an inherent part of practically every task or project we do in life. The interrelationship among these three concepts is illustrated in Figure 5.

The Foundation of Empowerment

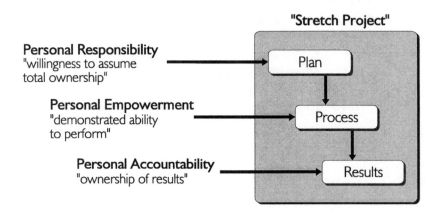

Figure 5. The interrelationship between personal responsibility, accountability, and empowerment as
applied to a project or task.

When assigned a project or a task, the detail and inclusive-
ness of planning is directly proportional to one's "willingness to assume total responsibility," before one does anything. This mindset determines whether the plan will be
well thought out taking into account unforeseen contingen-
cies, or superficial and subject to unpleasant surprises. The
level and quality of performance, as a process, is primarily
determined by how well we have performed in the past —
personal empowerment. Where the requirements of the project or task require greater competence than has been previously demonstrated, the successful performance of the project or task simultaneously results in expanded personal
empowerment. When the project or task is completed, per-

sonal accountability simply means claiming ownership of the results, without reasons and/or excuses. In order to practice empowerment, these three concepts have to be learned as *functional skills*. The following exercise illustrates the process which you will need to practice in order to become skilled at using these concepts.

An Empowerment Exercise

When empowerment is first implemented, the most difficult competency employees experience is self-management. Very few employees already know how to plan, organize, execute, and focus their work responsibilities. Therefore, we have chosen self-management skills to illustrate this skills-building exercise.

Using the definitions discussed for personal responsibility, accountability, and empowerment, generate applications of each of these concepts to a task or project where professional development will be required.

Step 1: Personal Responsibility

What is the opportunity for expanded personal empowerment?

Learn the skills necessary for responsible self-management.

Step 2: Personal Empowerment

What new mindset, skills, and competencies do I need to learn to become self-managed?

1. Determine the self-management skills I need most to learn:

i.   100 percent personal responsibility and accountability for my job. (Cognitive skill)

ii. Planning and organizing. (Functional skills)

iii. Execution of and focus on tasks. (Functional skills)

2. Acquire a mentor to coach me and hold me accountable for the application of these skill sets to a stretch project.

3. Attend one internal or external seminar per month on each of the skill sets above over the next three months.

4. Actively solicit co-workers' evaluations of the three skill sets every three months until an outstanding performance level is achieved.

Step 3: Personal Accountability

How do I measure or evaluate the achievement of the new skill sets I need to learn?

1. Use my organization's diagnostic instruments and facilitator feedback to ensure that the three self-management skills sets cited in Step 2 show measured improvement.

2. By a given date, I will have a mentor to oversee and evaluate my progress in mastering the three self-management skill sets cited in Step 2.

3. Report to my mentor the summarized new learnings acquired from each of the skill-based seminars.

4. Track my three-month interval progress by co-workers until an outstanding performance evaluation is achieved.

Notice that each of the personal accountability measures are directly tied to the personal empowerment actions. The essence of the actions for personal empowerment is summarized by the question, what new mindset, skills, and competencies must I learn in order to successfully execute this task or project? In a like manner, the summarized question for personal accountability is, in what ways could I hold myself and others *unquestionably* accountable for having accomplished this task or project? This requirement is, by far, the most difficult and challenging to master as a functional skill. The extent to which empowerment will ultimately work depends on the courage of the change agents to practice this skill, *with integrity*. We repeat, for emphasis, holding self and others accountable is key to the successful implementation of empowerment.

Use the format below and on the following page to practice this exercise in an area of professional growth that is of interest to you.

Step 1: Personal Responsibility

What is an area for improvement or what is an opportunity for expanded empowerment?

Step 2: Personal Empowerment

What new mindset, skills, and competencies must I acquire to accomplish this project?

1.

2.

3.

4.

5.

Step 3: Personal Accountability

How can I hold myself accountable for having achieved the items in Step 2?

1.

2.

3.

4.

5.

By repeatedly practicing this three-step process for your personally chosen stretch projects, personal responsibility, accountability, and empowerment will become functional skills. As you proceed through a day, notice how this three-step process characterizes practically everything you do.

As you begin to practice this three-step process, you will be challenged by your old way of thinking. The challenge is to keep you where you are and prevent the professional growth process. What you will be reminded of is that change invariably involves moving beyond a personal barrier — personal growth. The following chapter discusses the relationship between personal empowerment and personal growth.

Chapter 6. **Personal Empowerment — A Personal Growth Process**

♦ Introduction

Most writings on empowerment rarely, if ever, discuss the relationship between personal empowerment and personal growth, yet the two are interdependent. We even attempt to separate our life experiences into personal and professional. This attempted separation is artificial and we should acknowledge it. Granted, the settings are different, but the scenarios are strikingly similar. For example, many of us believe that if we are aware of a bias we have, we can actually drop it off at the door-sill of work and pick it up again at the end of the day — and no harm is done during the day. Not so! Each of us is one integrated individual. Each of us brings our total system of beliefs and behaviors everywhere we are. We simply behave in more subtle ways when it is unacceptable to behave in a more overt manner. This dimension of personal growth is interpersonal. The other dimension of personal growth which determines our level of professional performance is intrapersonal — that is, the extent to which we have engaged self-introspection to discover self-limiting beliefs relating to our full performance capacity. The ability to live up to our full potential, as well as to work productively with others, is dependent upon how well we have resolved intrapersonal and interpersonal issues, respectively. In this chapter, we will examine the relationship between personal empowerment and personal growth and offer suggestions about how to engage the personal growth process at a personally appropriate pace.

♦ Personal Growth and Empowerment

When we discussed the progression of responsibility scales on page 47, we did not go into detail as to how this process actually occurs. This discussion will show how personal growth is related to greater personal responsibility and accountability. Personal growth is the result of a change in perception about our capability to deal with life. This change usually begins with the discovery of a self-limiting belief. When such a belief is challenged and reexamined, we often discover that it is not valid. This insight is called a realization.

Several years ago, I (BG) served as a mentor to one of our newly hired employees. I could see that he was quite talented, but I detected that he was reluctant to take full charge of projects for which I believed he was capable. His performance was excellent by comparison to other employees — about 85 percent on the responsibility scale. However, he would never exceed this percentage by coming up with an idea that would make him fully responsible if he thought it would be exposed to critical review. You have probably already picked up the area of his self-limiting belief — rejection. In a conversation with me, he confided that he had always gotten by with 85 percent effort because he was so naturally talented. He had always believed that, if you take chances (with something really new and different), it will probably be rejected. He also had solid evidence dating back to a grammar school incident where red grass and green cows were not acceptable to his teacher. We discussed whether or not the decision he made then should still limit his performance today. He never answered that question to me verbally, but in the following weeks, I could begin to see a dramatic shift in his work in terms of risk taking. That belief was beginning to play a minimal role in the way he began to take ownership of projects in spite of the chalenges to which they were exposed.

This is the process by which an individual moves along the responsibility scale to achieve a greater capacity to perform. We can begin to see that every time we achieve a breakthrough in personal growth, we simultaneously become more personally empowered.

As long as we design our lives to remain in comfort-zone situations, such issues relating to our performance rarely surface. In high-involvement management systems, intrapersonal and interpersonal issues are an integral part of the operation and are rarely avoidable. They invariably surface quickest in the formation of new teams, as described in the following example of interpersonal conflict.

A major R&D organization, implementing empowerment, put into operation several self-directed teams across exempt/non-exempt lines. Exempt employees are salaried, whereas non-exempt employees work on an hourly basis. In many organizations there is a strong bias against non-exempt employees by exempt employees in terms of ability and competence. In the initial stages of operation, most of the non-exempt team members acquiesced to the strong suggestions of exempt employees and managers. Productivity gradually began to fall, in spite of the fact that the improvement projections showed an increase of 50 percent as teams. When breakdown forced a heated team discussion, what surfaced were biased beliefs and attitudes about inferiority/superiority, elitism/classism, formal education/ on-the-job learning, and a general lack of mutual respect among team members. The team spent the next three months resolving these issues while progressively approaching their projected level of productivity.

At the heart of the team's transformation was the personal growth they collectively experienced. In this case, the team was forced to deal with sensitive issues they would have preferred to ignore. The learning from this example is to anticipate dimensions of diversity and to have a plan to proactively resolve them before they become issues for resolution. As teaming becomes increasingly necessary, issues such as diversity and trust will have to be resolved before teams can become productive, particularly those which are self-directed. An important part of constructively working with other human beings is the personal change we need to make in order to have compatible relationships. The next section discusses how personal growth is an integral part of life, whether we voluntarily engage it or not.

Personal Growth

At a much less intense level, we are continually learning life's little lessons through our daily array of interpersonal interactions that might be called "the workshop of life." The workshop of life is a personal growth process in which everyone is engaged — some consciously, but most of us unconsciously. Personal growth is the sum total of our day-to-day experiences that result in our gradual lifelong process of learning and maturing. We enrolled in this workshop at birth and we will be engaged in it until death.

The experience which results from this lifelong process of expanded empowerment is transformation. In simple terms, transformation is the invalidation of conflict-producing, counterproductive, and/or self-limiting beliefs. The essential nature of transformation is that it is irreversible and comprehensive in every aspect of our lives. Since we rarely understand ourselves at the level of our most deeply hidden beliefs, *conflict and/or limited performance are life's feedback signals to let us know we are being driven or limited by one of these subliminal beliefs.* We tend to interpret this feedback as something is wrong with someone else or some situation external to us. Therefore, we generally transform by an almost imperceptible evolutionary process — except when we experience a significant crisis or illness. These experiences tend to involuntarily slingshot us into expanded maturity and a more harmonious adjustment to life.

Consider Allen, a manager who, after many years, began to notice that he continually had difficulties with individuals who did not appear to be working all the time. Completing a task early and taking a break, or taking time to chat with a co-worker was interpreted by Allen as wasting time or just plain laziness. Naturally, he would intervene with corrective action, which worsened already strained working relationships. Then, in the course of a relationship training, Allen was facilitated in rediscovering a phrase his mother often repeated and which he had obviously adopted, "Idle hands are the devil's workshop." That phrase, coupled with his Protestant-ethic upbringing, had become not only a *guiding* principle, but a *driving* principle in his life. He applied it not only to himself, but unconsciously to others whom he managed. This realization was a breakthrough which totally changed his ability to give up control. Allen developed a new dimension to his management style — focusing on results and productivity while exerting less control over an individual's style and the details of the process.

The relationship of Allen's personal breakthrough to empowerment was his newly found ability to continually minimize the necessity for management and maximize his focus on proactive accountability. This behavior began to show up, not only in the workplace but also in his personal life.

♦ Engaging the Process of Personal Empowerment

A less stressful way to become personally empowered, as an ongoing process, begins with the conscious acknowledgment and acceptance that personal growth is an inherent part of the human condition. Then becoming aware of the myriad of ways to proactively engage the process, both in personal and professional situations. The guiding criterion is that the process or method used is *personally appropriate* and fits you.

The least confrontational means of engaging the process of personal growth is by reading books and listening to tapes on self-improvement, followed by conversations with people with whom you feel comfortable. In order to more actively engage the process, you might utilize the variety of personal development courses and seminars offered by your organization in both intrapersonal and interpersonal skills. Basic courses in intrapersonal skills involve self-responsibility and accountability, stress management, time/life management, and decision making. Whereas those in interpersonal skills involve problem solving, relationships, communication, and organizational management. More advanced offerings in personal development involve diversity, leadership, creativity, and quantum-thinking (chapter 15). If your organization does not make such courses readily available, you have a personal responsibility to acquire personal development with your own resources. After all, it is an investment in your future, even though your company may also have an obligation that it is either unable or unwilling to fulfill. In summary, personal empowerment — the process — is synonymous with personal growth.

The following event illustrates how personal growth can literally transform the commitment of an executive to an initiative, when it is done in a personally appropriate manner.

> The CEO of Planedome Industries, Inc. preferred to work alone. He found it difficult to understand his human resource department's increasing demands for empowerment training for management. He had already authorized thousands of dollars for the quality initiative training. Why didn't people just do their jobs? Whatever happened to the good old-fashioned work ethic? When the empowerment consultant suggested that he go through a 360-degree assessment to determine his level of living and modeling empowerment behaviors, he resistantly agreed. When he had an opportunity to discuss challenging feedback in a private session, he began to view his involvement, behaviors, and commitment as viewed by others as central to the success of his company. He also began to view training as an important part of the education process for workers acquiring new knowledge. At the end of the session, he thanked the consultant for relieving a lot of his anxiety about change, high-involvement, and the need for knowledgeable employees.

A 360-degree assessment was obviously the best feedback mechanism for this CEO. It allowed him the freedom to control the process, the mode of feedback, and how seriously he considered the feedback. When this process is performed with a skillful facilitator, high-level executives are extremely receptive to profound change. This type of process can be of immense importance where organizations expend large sums of money and considerable employee training time in instituting new organizational initiatives.

The Role of Training

Training as we have traditionally known it is on the verge of a revolution. This revolution is being driven, most of all, by customers wanting training anytime and anywhere. They also want the most extensive application of training in the shortest time and at the least expense for the largest number of employees. All of these demands are now possible because of advancements in information technology. Specifically, computer-assisted learning (CAL) programs for both single-user and group modes are now being developed in a variety of areas. The CAL programs include video presentations, video scenarios, question-and-answer discussions, interactive case studies, and stepwise processes for learning self-management skills. The power of CAL is that by using interactive multimedia, learning occurs both consciously and unconsciously — that is, we remember proactive behaviors without the need for conscious recall, such as encouraging the improvement of an employee rather than reprimanding.

We use the term *training* to include education, skills development, and organizational transformation where change initiatives are involved. Change initiatives typically include education and organizational transformation. Examples of change initiatives are those illustrated in the diagram on page 25. Workshops and seminars in these areas are still most effectively done in groups where the most powerful aspects of transformational technology can be preserved. These include team exercises, interactive discussions, and group facilitation.

As the United States has become more and more dominated by knowledge and service industries, it has become increasingly necessary to value new learning as an integral and ongoing part of doing business. Since we tend to be systems-oriented, we often ignore how vital people-oriented skills and competencies are in terms of productivity and the bottom line. The workplace phenomenon driving the need for continuous learning is the transition from the information era to the present knowledge-based era. New learning (or knowledge) is the result of the creative integration of information. We are beginning to understand that business competitiveness is based upon realizing that knowledgeable workers are the continuing source of new products and services. Thus, the key is to encourage and support self-motivated personal *and* professional growth.

Part II. Teamwork

And it is still true, no matter how old you are — when you go out into the world, it is best to hold hands and stick together.

**"All I Really Need to Know
I Learned in Kindergarten"
Robert Fulghum**

Chapter 7. **Team Empowerment**

♦ Introduction

We believe that teaming has increased in popularity over the past ten years because it is a crucial component in successfully implementing and sustaining high employee-involvement programs, such as Quality, Reengineering, ES&H, and Empowerment. The establishment of high-performance teams, which requires a high level of commitment to a group in preference to oneself, is very challenging to U. S. Americans. The reason is, the most fundamental core value of U. S. Americans is individualism, commonly expressed in terms of personal freedom, personal achievement, and personal reward. The necessities and benefits derived from teamwork far outweigh any reluctance we may have about fundamental change required to embrace teaming. Proven benefits resulting from teamwork are increased productivity, efficiency, quality, creativity, commitment, and a more decentralized organizational structure.[3]

Although many organizations view teaming as an initiative comparable to quality, we tend to view it as a means of implementing high-involvement. This view prevents the process of implementing teams unnecessarily, but as dictated by necessity, efficiency, or opportunity. In addition, our focus on individualism must be placed in perspective. Consider the point of view of Dr. Ronald Heifetz of the Kennedy School of Government at Harvard University:

> *We have an ideal of individualism — rugged individualism — embedded in our culture, and it truly is a wonderful thing. The notion of rugged individualism has given rise to a great deal*

> *of American ingenuity, creativity, enthusiasm,*
> *and values of integrity. But it has a downside*
> *when organizations believe that this capacity is*
> *going to work in complicated situations requir-*
> *ing the efforts, wisdom, and points of view of a*
> *lot of different people.*

In this chapter we will define the concept of team empowerment, outline the criteria for teams, discuss team empowerment leadership, and discuss the governing principles of
empowered teams.

◆ Team Empowerment

In general, a team is a collection of individuals who must
rely on group collaboration and support to experience success or achieve their goal. Typically, there are no redundant
roles, except in the case of large projects. The central idea
behind a team is that a strong collective approach is ultimately more powerful in consistently producing quality results than the efforts of a collection of individuals. This
collective approach is in preference to pitted competition
between individuals in the same organization.

Team empowerment is the capacity of a group of individuals
(a team) to operate in an independent manner in proportion
to their individual and collective skills and competencies.
A team which operates within or just beyond the limitations
of its performance capacity is an empowered team. The
greater the demonstrated skills and competencies, the
greater the autonomy. A basic premise of team empowerment is that the most productive team is realized by the
development of each team member through personal empowerment. For many organizations attempting to implement teaming, this basic premise is often missing. There-

fore, a particularly important element for empowered teams in their interdependent operation is the full expression of individual excellence. However, the prevailing premise is that no team member is more important than the team.

Designations of Empowered Teams

The degree of autonomy of operation in teams can vary significantly from "manager-directed teams" to "totally self-directed teams." This variation of operation is described by the five types of teams shown in Table 1. These distinctions can be very important. Without them, confusion often arises among team members as to how much direction they will or should have from management. These descriptions also provide the assignment of a team designation based upon clearly defined criteria. The central theme in these descriptions is the progressive increase of independent operation corresponding to increasing individual and team empowerment. As a team moves through the various designations corresponding to greater autonomy, the relinquishing of management and supervisory control is a key factor in the team's success.

The criteria in Table 1 also span the designations *special projects teams,* which correspond to (1) and (2), to *work teams*, which describe (4) and (5); (3) is in-between these two designations. We can easily see that special projects teams are more temporary and require less mastery of interpersonal and self-management skills. Whereas, work teams are more permanent and ultimately require considerable interpersonal and management mastery.

Table 1. Team Designations and Operations as a Function of Individual and Team Competence

Team Designation	Operation
1) Manager-Directed	Manager assigns the project and team members, and manages the team process in the traditional manner.
2) Manager-Participant	Manager selects the projects and becomes part of the team. Team operation is more egalitarian, but the manager has the final decision.
3) Manager-Facilitator	Manager and team members are selected by the nature of the project, i.e., cross-functional, quality, customer, etc. Manager is an equal team member, but is acknowledged to bring necessary facilitative skills to the egalitarian team operation.
4) Manager-Coordinator	Manager is not a team member. Team members are selected by the nature of the project. Team operates autonomously within specific guidelines. Manager assures quality, customer satisfaction, team objectives, and where necessary, coaching and mentoring.
5) Self-Directed	Little or no management involvement. Manager may act as a consultant. Team selects projects or tasks, is self-managed, and is held *accountable* for continuing to *earn* its independent operation. Continuous learning is a way of life.

Team Empowerment Requires Responsibility and Accountability

Team empowerment also implies that each team member is *simultaneously* 100 percent individually and 100 percent collectively responsible and accountable for the results produced by the team. Therefore, each team member has not only the obligation, but the responsibility, to hold himself or herself accountable for his or her performance, as well as the performance of the other team members. This is more easily said than done. It can be very risky to hold a team member accountable because it can only be credibly done if one is self-accountable. Accountability is probably the most challenging aspect of effectively implementing team empowerment. As a team progresses through the various designations in Table 1, team members begin to *experience* the reality of accountability to a progressively greater extent.

The following example illustrates the difficulties change-management teams commonly experience when they discover the transformation in mindset necessary to become committed to a change initiative. We discussed these shifts in thinking for an empowerment initiative on pages 27 through 30.

Manufacturing Technology, Inc. had embarked on its ISO 9000 certification process with fanfare and enthusiasm. The organization was capable of meeting the certification deadline established by its president, but it would require a stretch. The quality assurance coordinator brought technically capable individuals together from different areas of the company to form teams. He made roles and responsibilities clear as he delegated aspects of the certification.

He worked to make sure that everyone knew how what they were doing affected other teams in the certification process. As meetings took place over time, some teams began to experience interpersonal conflicts and blamed their lack of progress on inadequate resources and management control preventing them from making the changes they needed. The quality assurance coordinator could see that a new kind of mindset was going to be needed — a mindset which emphasized individual and collective ownership for the success of each team as well as the overall process.

He decided to reestablish basic agreements which he assumed already existed:

1) Acceptance of the necessity for the certification.

2) Confirmation that the goal was compelling.

3) Alignment with and ownership of the certification process.

4) Provision for basic needs and resources.

5) Commitment to the purpose and the goal.

6) Establishment of a team acknowledgment/reward system.

It is not uncommon when change-management teams are struggling with their own commitment to fundamental change to view external support as their source of difficulty. The dominant focus in such cases is on how external systems and leadership are not supportive, even when this may not be the case. Leadership's role is to restate the objectives and business rationale, and allow the teams the opportunity to face the reality of commitment. Commitment is ultimately confirmed when the challenge of greatest difficulty is successfully overcome. Commitment is commonly determined *after* a process begins, regardless of verbal declarations made initially.

♦ Criteria for Team Efforts

Team empowerment allows a team approach to the achievement of an objective when necessary *and* an individual approach when a team effort is unnecessary or inappropriate. Organizations operating at the far right of Figure 1 (page 8), such as W. L. Gore and Associates, TDIndustries, and Brown & Root, are dominated by teamwork. Very little, if any, of their activity involving a whole piece of work is an individual effort. Most organizations such as EDS, Amoco, and Martin Marietta Energy Systems incorporate a combination of individual contribution and teamwork as is necessary, efficient, or opportunistic.

Team efforts are more appropriate than individual efforts when:

1) No one person has all the information or expertise to accomplish the objective or goal within a given time frame.

2) There is a need, benefit, or value to working across disciplines or divisions.

3) Several or many points of view are necessary to solve difficulties or problems relating to the objective or goal.

4) A group naturally prefers a team-oriented approach *and* productivity and employee well-being are not compromised.

5) There is a necessity (or opportunity) for greater productivity, quality, and competitive advantage through team synergism.

It is important to note that each of these criteria falls into the category of necessity, efficiency, or opportunity (or a combination).

Guillory and Galindo

◆ Team Empowerment Leadership

The more empowered a team is in utilizing a combination of its individual competencies, the less necessity there is for directed individual leadership; what emerges is *participative leadership*. Leadership takes on a completely different meaning in empowered organizations. If team members are self-motivated and self-directed, there is no need to lead in the traditional sense. Leadership may change constantly depending upon the situation the team might be experiencing. Most often, team members are not at the same level of personal empowerment. When teams are first formed, they are sometimes so focused on egalitarian operation that they fail to take advantage of experienced team members. When experienced individuals are utilized for their insights or expertise, the teaming process can be measurably accelerated. For example, such individuals are often knowledgeable of the crisis points teams go through and are able to place such crises in perspective relative to the team's importance. As the team develops as a cohesive group, participative leadership and egalitarian operation naturally emerge. The principles that govern empowered teams in their progressive development are summarized in the next section.

◆ Principles of Team Empowerment

1) *The team is principally (if not totally) self-directed.*

An empowered team assumes maximum responsibility and accountability for planning and implementing their tasks or projects in proportion to their demonstrated ability to perform. As the team's competency and level of performance increase, their freedom to operate independently increases proportionately ideally to complete self-management.

94

2) *Individual excellence is maximized within an interdependent network.*

Individual excellence is an integral part of full self-expression and should be encouraged *within* an interdependent network. This principle assumes that the team's performance capacity is in direct proportion to the collective capacity of its individual team members. However, this capacity is *only* realized when no team member is considered more important than the team, and they work to create synergy.

3) *Personal responsibility, accountability, and empowerment are maximized.*

Expanding one's personal responsibility, accountability, and empowerment is a continual process of personal development, which serves to maximize one's professional performance. The greater the ownership of these three personal characteristics, the more fully one's capacity to perform is realized (see Figure 5 on page 68).

4) *The team code of conduct governs expected team behavior.*

Empowered teams *require* a code of conduct which applies equally to all team members, irrespective of an individual's ability to perform in an exceptional manner. This code serves to set guidelines of expected behavior for enhancing the synergism of the team's performance.

5) *Trust, cooperation, and participative leadership are valued.*

Fundamental values common to empowered teams include the team members' willingness to foster a context of trust, cooperation, and rotating leadership roles based upon their various competencies. These essential values are key elements of the code of conduct.

For example, a diversity team from the ENSERCH Corporation created the following code of conduct:

- **Sensitivity** — We will, as a team, be sensitive to each other by practicing awareness, understanding, patience, and acceptance.

- **Accountability** — We will, as a team and individually, be dependable and responsive, and honor **all** our agreements.

- **Relationship** — We will, as a team, be committed to relationships which are genuine and supportive.

- **Equality** — We will, as a team, interact as equal partners for the overall success of the team, regardless of position or rank within the organization.

- **Communication** — We will, as a team, commit to open, honest communication — actively listening for new ideas and direction.

- **Respect** — We will value the diversity of our team, demonstrating respect by consistently maintaining confidentiality and nonjudgmental attitudes.

6) *Mastery of interpersonal skills and competencies is valued.*

When empowered teams are comprised of highly competent individuals, interpersonal dynamics emerge as the limiting factor to team performance. In fact, the extent to which a team can self-facilitate interpersonal compatibility is the extent to which they will ultimately realize their full potential. Mastery of this potential is therefore the limiting factor which determines whether a team progresses to the self-directed stage.

7) *Diversity is valued.*

Diversity is manifested in the myriad ways teams are put together. Examples include multicultural teams (necessary for global competitiveness), cross-functional teams (important to customer service and product development), and self-directed teams (critical to quality improvement). Dimensions of diversity (such as race, sex, ethnicity, culture, workstyle, and age) play a major role in the efficient operation and ultimate success of empowered teams.

8) *Alignment with and commitment to the team's strategies, objectives, and goals are necessities.*

A team is not a team (empowered or not) until team members are clearly aligned and their commitment to strategies, objectives, and goals is unquestionably established. If any perception of a question exists (even from an intuitive feeling), it should be brought up for discussion and resolution. If put off, it will later emerge with greater counterproductive intensity.

When a project, task, or work process has been identified as a team effort and the team members are selected, the implementation process begins. A unique approach to this process is discussed in the following chapter.

Chapter 8. Implementing Team Empowerment

♦ Introduction

The best place to begin implementing team empowerment is with existing teams. However, the guidelines described throughout this chapter apply equally to start-up teams. We will discuss the following subjects in this chapter: team implementation, the team empowerment process, the empowerment spiral, the stepwise process of implementing team empowerment, and team evaluations.

♦ Team Implementation

Implementing team empowerment usually begins by responding to three key questions:

1) What areas of responsibility could a team perform more productively with the least amount of control or direction?

   These areas may fall into two categories:

   i) those responsibilities which the team is already capable of handling and require the least amount of coaching.

   ii) those responsibilities which would be a stretch and require significant coaching, new learning, and very specific guidelines.

2) What new mindsets, skills, and competencies must the team acquire, individually and collectively, in or-

der to perform the new expanded responsibilities at a customer-demanded level of expectation?

3) How could the team members hold themselves unquestionably accountable for having learned the new mindsets, skills, and competencies, *and* for having successfully performed the task or project at the level of customer expectation or beyond?

These requirements are best established *before* the project or task begins and should have definitive metrics (or measurables) involved in the evaluation. The more specific and definable the accountability measures, the more successful the process *and* the project. The more nebulous the accountability measures, the more confusing and less effective the process and the less likely the success of the project.

After responding to the three questions above, an area of expanded responsibility for self-direction should be identified. In addition, new learning and accountability measures should be clearly defined. The team composition is defined on the basis of the expertise demanded by the task, project, or work process.

The following example illustrates the application of this sequence of questions for a customer-focused service team.

A Team Empowerment Example

Responsibility: What is the opportunity for expanded team empowerment?

Develop a strategically aligned, customer-focused service team.

Empowerment: What new skills, competencies, and principles do we need to learn? Or, how are we going to do it?

1) Create a code of conduct or team value system.

2) Align our team's activities with the customer's organizational or business unit vision.

3) Add value and/or profitability to the customer we are serving.

4) Evaluate and address the need for continuous team learning in order to provide quality service for the customer.

5) Be knowledgeable of the cutting-edge opportunities in alignment with serving the customer.

Accountability: How do we measure or evaluate the elements of our new learning?

1) Brainstorming session: What characteristics are absolutely necessary to have a customer-focused service team that exceeds customer expectations? Select the top five characteristics and define them. Examples often include trust, commitment, communication, relationships, and diversity (see page 96).

2) Evaluate if our activities are in alignment with our customer's goals (short-term or long-term).

3) Determine or calculate how our activities increase the efficiency or profitability of our customer's operation.

4) Do in-house team training where necessary and track progress with well-known diagnostic instruments to

measure our progress. Do regular customer-service surveys to track our quantitative progress.

5) Appoint a rotating team member to collect information relative to up-to-date advances in the areas of interest of the service team's activities. Have a team evaluation of the implementation and effectiveness of this continuous-learning process.

♦ The Team Empowerment Process

Having identified a stretch project, task, or work process and a preliminary team, the team empowerment process proceeds by the team responding to the following set of guidelines:

1) **Define the purpose of the team.**

   • Why does the team exist?
   • What is the team's objective or goal?

2) **Define the roles and responsibilities of the team.**

   • Is each team member clear about her or his role?
   • Does each team member know the roles of the other team members?
   • Does the team have all the expertise necessary? If not, then how will the team utilize existing organizational expertise and support that is lacking among team members?

3) **Define the mode of operation of the team.**

   • Establish a working vocabulary for important terms (page 234).
   • Establish a mode of leadership and an accountability system.

- Discuss team trust, relationship, communication, support, commitment, etc.
- Establish a team code of conduct or value system.
- Decide on a team operating designation as defined by Table 1 (page 90).

4) **Select a manager to coach and set guidelines for the team.**

- Manager and team should agree on guidelines.
- Manager and team should establish accountability in terms of quality, productivity, and team functioning.
- Manager should coach as necessary.
- Manager should provide the necessary resources for the team to experience success.
- Manager and team are clear on overall team responsibility and accountability, what support the team will receive from the organization, and what specific authority the team has to meet their objective.

5) **Utilize training as an integral part of team empowerment.**

- Take training to understand and use team empowerment.
- Training in technical, organizational, and interpersonal skills must be an ongoing part of the process.
- Integrate just-in-time training into the process as required (e.g., interpersonal skills, coaching, and holding others accountable).

6) **Proceed to function with established management accountability checkpoints.**

- Assess team operation and objectives shortly after beginning.

- Assess team operation and objectives at half completion.
- Use crisis as an opportunity for a breakthrough.
- Assess team success at completion.

7) **Evaluate team performance at completion.**

- What worked?
- What did not work?
- What did we learn for future teams?
- What do we need to learn for future teams?
- Establish a new team project (with fewer guidelines) and "go for it!"

The difficulty in implementing teaming is not how or what to do. There are literally hundreds of descriptions — all probably valid. The challenge really comes in execution. Several years ago, we formed a Quality Performance Team to oversee our organization's quality program. The initial problem we had was defining quality. We all knew quality when we saw it, but defining it for all of the organizational functions was another matter. After much discussion, we finally agreed on the following three-part definition:

Quality is:

- An attitude of service and continuous improvement.

- Performance which reflects the highest available efficiency of processes and procedures.

- Confirmed by specific measurable and definable results which exceed the expectations of internal and external customers.

As we struggled through the process of defining quality, we had two important realizations. First, we did not operate according to this definition. Second, by adopting this definition, we were each declaring our own commitment to a new performance standard. We later understood that our struggle was about our two realizations and not about our ability to define quality.

Our second problem occurred when we were attempting to agree on how we would begin *enforcing* quality measures where employees were concerned. Team members' friendships would be strained, resistance would be inevitable, and there was concern that some employees would simply choose to ignore us. These issues created significant discord within the team. We began experiencing the crisis of teaming; that is, we were unknowingly deciding if the team would survive. One member of our team found the give-and-take sufficiently stressful that she decided to leave the team. It became obvious that each of us would have to give up something important about the way we operated as individuals in order for the team to be successful. Each of us made that commitment by declaring that we would deal with any conflict or dysfunctional behavioral pattern that blocked the team's progress. Amazingly, everything began to crystallize. The weeks of apparent floundering was precisely the process we needed to go through to *find* ourselves. We became a powerful force for continuous improvement and change in our organization.

It is interesting how team processes take on their own lives. Those teams which are required to move beyond temporary projects (project teams) will inevitably experience, in one way or another, the same process we experienced. What we discovered were two important lessons. First, the human capacity to achieve extraordinary performance standards is unquestioned. Second, the human *willingness* to give up self-interest in the best interest of a group can be a significant struggle. Repetitively accepting this type of challenge and succeeding is the essence of the empowerment spiral, which is depicted on this book's front cover.

◆ The Empowerment Spiral

At the successful completion of each task or project where a stretch has been involved, the team acquires a greater capacity to perform independently: ΔE (read "delta E", this symbol denotes a quantum jump in empowerment). This capacity is evaluated jointly by the manager or team leader and the team as a basis for establishing expanded guidelines for future team operation. This evaluation process is often skipped. To be a continuous-learning organization requires that, at the completion of team projects, time be taken to debrief. It is not unusual to feel that there is no time for more meetings. But when it comes to discussing what was learned from the team experience, it is absolutely necessary to take time to reflect. This is the most effective way for a team to evaluate its expanded ability to perform on future assigned projects.

The empowerment spiral (hereafter referred to as the *spiral*) represents the measurable or demonstrated ability of the team to perform at or above customer expectation. Thus, Figure 6 shows a continuing process of expanded team empowerment (ΔEs). The dots represent starts and endpoints of a stretch project. The solid line semicircle represents the stretch process from beginning to end. ΔE ($E_{final\ state}$ - $E_{initial\ state}$) is the increased capability of the team, both individually and collectively. The spiral is represented by successively larger circles (combination of solid and dotted semicircles). As the spiral becomes progressively larger, the team assumes more responsibility for self-selection of projects and self-management. The ultimate state of team empowerment is total self-direction.

106

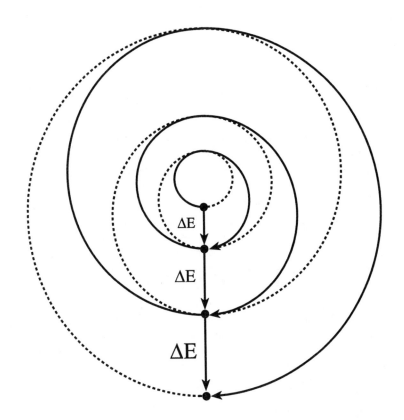

The Empowerment Spiral

Figure 6. The empowerment spiral represents a series of
stretch projects which continually expand the
empowerment of an individual or a team.

Guillory and Galindo

The following example illustrates the initial enthusiasm and subsequent reality that work teams experience when they begin to understand the challenging new learning necessary for self-management.

> "We are going to organize ourselves into teams and each team will have a team leader," announced the product development manager. It sounded good to Maria. "Now maybe we can focus on one thing to completion," she thought. As their first project began, it became increasingly clear that the team leader needed specific guidelines beyond ready, set, go! What sounded like a good idea became chaotic and business as usual. When the manager realized how errant the process had become, he sought out a facilitator to help him and the team get back on track. Although it was tedious at first, the team settled into a clearly defined process of implementing team empowerment that produced measurably better results. It soon became clear that teaming was going to be a challenging process of learning new responsibilities and skills. The most challenging to Maria's team were interpersonal and administrative skills, as well as being directly responsible for meeting customers' expectations. At times her team wondered whether it was what they *really* wanted. What kept them going, in spite of their doubts, was the realization that teaming was significantly more powerful in expanding their unit's productivity, and that it was here to stay.

♦ Stepwise Process of Implementing Team Empowerment

In this sequential process of *initiating* team empowerment, the manager and team leader may be the same person. In addition, we recommend that the titles used be adapted to your organization's language. We have learned from experience that the most important elements of implementing teamwork are clarity and appropriateness of functions.

The following steps describe the process for implementing team empowerment:

1) Manager assigns a specific project with a due date to a team of typically 5-10 individuals (appointed or self-selected). Team leader determines the level of individual and group responsibility and accountability and makes sure each member understands his or her individual and team roles. Team leader is also responsible for making sure all group members have the necessary skills.

Management Intervention One (MI-1)

Manager consults with team leader about individual and group responsibility and accountability. If needed, an Empowerment Assessment can be conducted to assess levels of individual and team empowerment.

2) Team creates a plan for successfully accomplishing the assigned project by proposing increased authority and greater opportunity for decision making.

Management Intervention Two (MI-2)

Manager reviews proposal in light of individual and team levels of empowerment. Manager and team jointly decide what level of decision-making authority will be allowed and clearly agree on the expanded boundaries and responsibilities of the team. Manager and team jointly agree on how to proceed.

3) Team leader or manager works closely with team members in the early stages of the project, providing necessary mentoring, coaching, and feedback. Both the team leader and manager should be careful not to undermine newly granted authority. In some cases, management should allow teams to be unsuccessful rather than intervening. This can provide a critical

learning experience and should be viewed as an investment in future success.

Management Intervention Three (MI-3)

At one-fourth completion, manager evaluates the team's progress, focusing on results, not process. Manager emphasizes customer satisfaction and needs and the necessity for meeting jointly established deadlines.

4) Team has regular meetings (at least once a week) to determine both individual and team progress. The team process depends on the willingness of individuals to hold each other accountable without the necessity for management intervention.

Management Intervention Four (MI-4)

The team leader or manager should facilitate the team in an evaluation of each other's performance. Manager should coach highly empowered team members and the team leader on how to coach others. Manager coaches marginally performing team members to assume expanded responsibility.

5) The manager evaluates progress at the halfway point. If there is marginal performance, the manager proactively (nonpunitively) holds the team accountable for results and provides an opportunity for the team to resolve difficulties without management intervention. If this is unsuccessful, the manager must facilitate the team, incorporating whatever degree of empowerment possible.

Management Intervention Five (MI-5)

Manager provides leadership by showing the team how crisis is an opportunity for growth. Manager uses breakdowns to teach empowerment principles and, if needed, facilitates the learning of interpersonal skills. If necessary, the manager may want to consider additional training or using an in-house or outside human-resource consultant.

6) Once the difficulty has been overcome, the team proceeds with the project, striving for greater quality, service, and productivity by incorporating lessons learned from the breakdown. Team members hold a brainstorming session on how they can improve the final product or service and *exceed* customer expectations.

Management Intervention Six (MI-6)

Manager offers support and asks the team what resources they require in order to successfully complete the project. Manager should be prepared to meet their requests. This helps establish a new context for manager-employee relationships based on empowerment and trust.

7) As the project nears completion, the team identifies how they have met or exceeded originally established objectives through personal and team empowerment.

Management Intervention Seven (MI-7)

Manager acknowledges successes of the team and appropriately rewards the members. This is also an opportune time to review the empowerment vocabulary so that it becomes integrated into the organizational culture.

8) Team successfully completes the project.

Management Intervention Eight (MI-8)

Manager calls a meeting with all team members. This is an opportunity to openly discuss the successes and drawbacks of the entire process. Topics could include new interpersonal skills that were developed, as well as targeting future training needs. Manager and team discuss how to improve the process in the future. If appropriate, utilize written team evaluations.

♦ Team Evaluations

At the completion of your team task or project, you might use the following two evaluation exercises in order to maximize your learning and establish team objectives for the next task or project.

Exercise One

In the first exercise, each team member individually responds to each Yes or No question below, based upon his or her experience of the team's performance. At the completion, Yes and No responses for each question are compared and discussed by the team. Where there is disagreement, the discussion should involve where breakdown occurred and how it might be avoided in the future.

TEAM EVALUATION

		YES	NO
1)	Did you decide each person's role and responsibilities based upon what she or he was most skilled at doing or learning?	—	—
2)	Were you clear about your role and responsibilities in the task or project *before* you began the implementation process?	—	—
3)	Did your team *avoid* repetition of process and ensure quality because *each team member* had a high degree of quality awareness and performance?	—	—
4)	Did your team utilize each team member in the *most effective manner*, by not having two or more people working on a one-person task or compensating for a team member's lack of performance?	—	—
5)	Did your team prepare, *as best it could*, during the planning phase, for implementing the project?	—	—
6)	Did you personally experience minimal interpersonal conflict or irritation in performing your responsibilities interdependently with your team members?	—	—
7)	Based upon your team's performance, did you work as effectively *as possible* as an empowered team (based upon your initial team competence?)	—	—
8)	Did your team's leadership style encourage maximum self-direction and team trust?	—	—

Exceptional success for the team in this evaluation exercise is realized when team members unanimously respond Yes to each of the eight questions.

Exercise Two

We previously stated that "A basic premise of team empowerment is that the most productive team is realized by the development of each team member through personal empowerment." The reason the following exercise is so important is that it provides an opportunity to receive pleasant and not-so-pleasant feedback that can enhance one's personal performance. Being receptive to such feedback involves overcoming barriers to personal growth. This is precisely the process of becoming more personally empowered.

To use the exercise on the following page, each team member evaluates himself or herself in the "Self" column, according to his or her team performance. Select the most prominent characteristics by not checking more than 15 of the 29 available. Then, write in the characteristic he or she believes would most improve his or her team performance in the (1) blank space.

Each team member then evaluates every other team member in terms of his or her perceived team performance, again selecting the most prominent characteristics (not more than 15). It is not necessary to have proof or an explanation for selecting a characteristic for another team member. Use your intuition or perceptions as feedback of your experience. Again, write in the characteristic you believe would most benefit each team member in his or her team performance in the blank space.

TEAM PARTICIPATION INTERACTION
How Do Others Perceive Us?

Personality Characteristic	Self					
1. *write in*						
2. trusting						
3. leadership						
4. reserved						
5. commitment						
6. creative						
7. arrogant						
8. values others						
9. sensitive						
10. supportive						
11. demanding						
12. understanding						
13. persistent						
14. intelligent						
15. communicates openly						
16. aggressive						
17. accepting of others						
18. domineering						
19. impatient						
20. unmovable						
21. sense of humor						
22. risk-taker						
23. cooperative						
24. emotional						
25. responsible						
26. knowledgeable						
27. intuitive						
28. flexible						
29. interdependent						

At the completion of the team "Self and Others" evaluation, create a process for each team member to receive feedback from every other team member for all 29 characteristics. For example, for a five-person team, an individual team member may receive any number from 0 to 4 for any of the characteristics listed. She or he may also receive several recommendations (write-in characteristics) for functioning more effectively as a team member from number (1).

The frequency of a specific characteristic provides valuable feedback as to how a team member is perceived by the group. Each of these can be compared with how an individual perceives herself or himself. This comparison is sometimes surprising to a team member and leads to new awareness and learning from the feedback. Finally, the characteristics most frequently selected by team members for an individual can be compared with the important team-building characteristics shown below. (The numbers correspond to those in the exercise.)

Important Team-Building Characteristics

2)	Trusting	12)	Understanding
3)	Leadership	15)	Communicates openly
5)	Commitment	17)	Accepting of Others
6)	Creative	23)	Cooperative
8)	Values Others	25)	Responsible
9)	Sensitive	28)	Flexible
10)	Supportive	29)	Interdependent

The *lack* of acknowledgment by the group of any of these characteristics provides a specific area of new learning or competence for each team member to master.

Beyond empowered teams, there exists a team performance level which exceeds the sum of the team members' talents. This performance level is called *synergism*. The requirements for synergism are discussed in the following chapter.

Chapter 9. Beyond Team Empowerment — Synergism

♦ Introduction

In the advanced stages of empowered team functioning, a new opportunity arises. The opportunity is to function at an even higher level of performance which goes beyond the sum of the team members' talents and abilities. This level of performance is called *synergism*. Synergism requires personal mastery, team creativity, individual and team learning, and systems thinking. Each of these subjects will be sequentially discussed in this chapter.

♦ Personal Mastery

The first requirement of a synergistic team is that the individual team members achieve a relatively high level of personal mastery. Personal mastery is the combination of a high level of self-actualization and professional competency. It is characteristic of individuals who "live their lives with passion and pursue their bliss," in the words of Joseph Campbell.[4] Life is a continual pursuit of excellence. In addition, the practice of introspective self-awareness is an ongoing process.

This individual makes a distinction between knowledge and wisdom. Knowledge is what one knows, whereas wisdom is one's *way of being*. Wisdom is what drives the humane application of knowledge in service to others. For example, an individual who has come to the *experiential* realization that all human beings are inherently equal would probably embrace diversity because it is the morally right thing to do, rather than requiring a foolproof business necessity.

However, the compatible business rationale is easily generated by responding to the following questions: Do I want to lead, manage, or participate within an organization which knowingly practices systematic exclusion of classes of employees? Do such practices violate my ethical beliefs of human behavior, even though they may be favorable to me? Finally, how much money is lost in terms of internal efficiency, motivation, creativity, and productivity by receiving limited but adequate output from excluded employees, while paying them full wages? If necessary, this amount is fairly easy to calculate by any good accountant, depending on a specific type of business.

In a like manner, individuals who feel an inherent connectedness to the earth and all its components would be morally motivated to protect people, animals, and the environment in the course of their business activities. Stringent legal requirements would only serve as guidelines for ethical practices rather than punitive measures for corrective abuses. The individual who engages personal mastery evolves a code of ethics which is sourced from wisdom. This code of ethics guides the moral behavior of this individual in such a way that a high level of personal integrity is maintained in relationship to people, animals, and the environment.

Personal mastery is most commonly played out by a team's code of conduct or value system. Most teams include the following team values: trust, communication, relationship, diversity, and alignment. Each of these values is uniquely defined and practiced by the team. Regardless of the specific code of conduct, the practical question is, how is a team member facilitated when she or he inevitably violates a team value? Personal mastery focuses on complete acceptance of the person while simultaneously requiring a team member's *commitment* to the team values in terms of ethics and behaviors. If an individual continually violates the team's values, it becomes necessary to evaluate his or her commitment and, correspondingly, whether the person should be part of the team. In this case, the evaluation is not based upon professional competency, but upon the degree of deviation of the individual's behavior from the team's code of conduct. For synergistic teams, team integrity is as or more important than individual competency. Individual competency is assumed to be a given.

Engaging personal mastery begins to move an individual to an expanded level of what it means to be human. One begins to blur the distinction between personal and professional to realize that we have one integrated moral code of ethics that applies everywhere. However, we may apply it differently to different people, depending on our unique biases and prejudices. Ultimately, the greatest challenge to continuing personal mastery is not the challenge of advanced professional competencies, but the unlimited development of self.

◆ Team Creativity

The second requirement of a synergistic team is the realization that team creativity supersedes individual creativity. The focused alignment of several individuals creates within the team a metalevel of creativity. This is commonly done by using a four-stage creative brainstorming process projected five to ten years into the future. The four stages are four segmented time periods (15-20 minutes each) in which the group progressively brainstorms ideas further and further from the present reality. Then they creatively connect these futuristic ideas back to the present mode of operation. The sequence of steps (ideas or products) provide the "stretch" goals for the team sourced from the team's synergism. The premise of the process is that the ideas generated by the team are at a higher level of creativity and challenge than would be possible for individuals alone.

The following example illustrates the process we commonly go through when presented with ideas beyond the present limits of our thinking.

When the challenge was first introduced to the group, Allen was positive he had the best solution, and worked to convince everyone to accept it. He felt himself growing resentful when someone suggested they all "look beyond the obvious" and go for a more creative approach. Everyone began to get excited about trying dream-state creativity. Allen thought about running away from the whole thing but decided that even though their methods were getting further out, this was the place to be to keep learning. At least he knew the old traditional creative methods were no longer as effective in his present fast-paced environment.

After several weeks of practice, the group was astounded by their abilities to collectively create new ideas having several dimensions of application. It appeared at times that they were able to create a mentally connected network of their individual creative ideas. The result was extraordinary creativity leading to their next-generation software program.

These situations provide us with opportunities for breakthroughs in our thinking, which typically lead to the next-generation products and services. We define such breakthroughs as quantum-thinking which we discuss in chapter 15. In general, quantum-thinking is the ability of the mind to operate at a metalevel of creativity. This ability is in direct proportion to the degree that one has successfully achieved personal mastery.

◆ Individual and Team Learning

The third requirement of synergism is an adopted mindset of continual individual and team learning (or collaborative learning) *as a way of life.* The greatest barrier to team learning is the individual and group resistance to overcoming self-imposed limitations rather than the ability to learn. Such limitations are so subtle that they are not consciously recognized by individuals and groups. This is why groups at this level of performance benefit measurably from regular external facilitation. The key to knowing whether such barriers exist is by the direct observation of results or by applying performance measures.

Individual and team learning occurs where the following interpersonal elements are present in the way the team functions:

1) Self-observation

2) Open communication

3) Suspension of assumptions

4) Dialogue

5) Consensus decision making

Self-Observation

Self-observation is the willingness to focus one's attention inwardly to one's own thoughts and feelings. If we view the outside environment (e.g., team functioning) as the source of a never-ending sequence of events (stimuli) which may or may not challenge the way we think, then those events which are in conflict with our beliefs instantly provoke feelings of threat (fear). Self-observation means that we have developed an ability to connect our feelings to our triggered belief, as the first step. And second, it means we have learned to honestly examine the validity of our triggered belief with respect to the external event. This process provides the opportunity for change and personal growth.

For example, self-directed team members are constantly in the process of balancing maximum self-direction and the need for a manager-coach during their growth process. The greater the extent to which their ego-drive for control can be set aside to honestly evaluate their proven competency as a team, the more productively the process of total self-direction can be accomplished. The same is true for the manager-coach in dealing with his or her ego-drive in giving up control to allow the team to set realistic stretch goals. The source of this element of synergistic team functioning is self-observation.

The following example illustrates how self-observation can eventually lead to a breakthrough in open communication.

Mark had never participated with a group where he was not in control. He had come from an academic background where results are everything and he was used to being ultimately responsible for getting them. In his heart he felt that no one was as dedicated or committed as he was. No one on the team appeared to put in the time or effort in continuous learning that he did. He eventually concluded that, in the final analysis, he could only depend on himself. The people around him consistently made mistakes and resisted feedback for doing things better.

As Maryanne experienced her teammate Mark, she wished she knew why he always appeared to be dissatisfied with the group's performance. He had a lot to contribute, but people were growing tired of his incessant attention to mistakes and the need for continuous improvement. It was hard to understand why someone like Mark, who expected perfection, would want to work with others.

Maryanne decided to learn more about his point of view and work toward a new level of team performance. She was confident that with open communication she could understand his point of view and begin to establish a win/win situation.

What they discovered is that conflicts are rarely, if ever, one-sided. Their righteous self-talk only served to stifle the team's growth. Maryanne's courage in creating the meeting with Mark was the breakthrough that came from self-observation of her own thoughts and feelings. The meeting with Mark provided the opportunity for the examination of the validity of their self-talk. Success in their discussion would depend on the second step of the process — open communication.

Open Communication

Open communication begins with the establishment of an environment where feelings, emotions, and widely diverging ideas can be expressed with little or no objection. Divergent ideas are simply viewed as part of the spectrum of discussion topics necessary to secure team alignment. It is important to recognize the fact that open communication is an ongoing process. As team members experience greater and greater team cohesiveness, barriers between and among themselves must necessarily be addressed.

For example, a sales team which had been together for three years began to experience a more difficult time reaching decisions which had previously been routine. One of the team members shared that she "experienced a sense of heaviness" in their meetings and felt that one of the team members was not being truthful with the team. When the accused team member gained sufficient courage, he finally admitted to the group that he no longer wanted to be in sales, and eventually left the group.

The point is this: In order to operate at peak performance as a team, there must be no hidden agendas. When necessary, team members must sometimes draw out someone who is stifled by his or her own reluctance to tell the truth.

The eventual result of not doing so will be some form of subtle (or not so subtle) sabotage as a prelude to leaving the team.

Suspension of Assumptions

Suspension of assumptions is the willingness to acknowledge that we unconsciously judge most everything we hear, and then to set aside our judgments. This ability connects to self-observation; by simply observing our mind's conversation about the matter at hand, we are free to more openly observe what someone else is proposing. This literally requires us to view the world through another's eyes or "walk in someone else's moccasins" (the original American Native saying). As an exercise, think of someone you disagreed with in a recent exchange of ideas. Project yourself into that person's mind. Imagine his or her childhood, history, family associations, education, and recent sequence of experiences. If you had that individual's history and present life situation, would you probably think like him or her? This sense of empathy can also be acquired by carefully observing someone's behavior in order to create an environment where his or her freedom of expression is maximized. By seeing the world through someone else's eyes, our judgments and assumptions are simultaneously suspended.

Dialogue

Dialogue is a state of team functioning where the flow, dynamics, and integration of ideas create synergism. In order for dialogue to occur, all of the previous elements of team learning must be present. For example, in a recent team discussion of how we might reengineer[5] the process for producing seminar workbooks, we all came to the conclusion that our discussion was about improving the existing process. This group realization provided the opportunity for us to see that we were avoiding the necessity of our own fundamental change for reengineering to occur, either in terms of our competence or new technological integration. This realization allowed the breakthrough to shift from *discussion* to *dialogue* around such questions as: How few hands need to touch the final seminar workbook? What new competencies, skills, and technology would be necessary for one person to do the entire process? What is lost in efficiency and new learning by having only one person handle the entire process? How do we optimally reengineer the process? The result of this dialogue went from ten pairs of hands in the process to three.

Consensus Decision Making

Consensus decision making is the process of creating committed alignment. It is the culmination of the elements discussed above. It may occur in a variety of ways, depending upon the situation. For example, when an expert is part of a team, it is not uncommon to defer to that individual's recommendation after sufficient team discussion and dialogue. On the other hand, most team decisions are made by a consensus process which takes into account a wide spectrum of viewpoints. This does not necessarily mean the final decision is an average of all points of view and certainly not a vote, but one which is simultaneously progressive *and* integrates the spectrum of differences expressed by the group. It ultimately integrates everyone's point of view into the final decision. This integration process is necessary for commitment.

Consensus is rarely achieved during a single meeting or discussion. It requires time for a team to internalize and process the various points of view. Quite often, the consensus process can create "third-way thinking" solutions — that is, solutions which are at a higher level of resolution than those under discussion.

Two years ago we were attempting to upgrade our creativity and innovation seminar. As we discussed the new techniques and methodologies available, we realized they were all within the present paradigm of thinking. We eventually concluded that the present paradigm was mature and offered no opportunities for new breakthroughs. We appeared to be at an impasse, since we had no previous experience with anticipating (or possibly being tuned to) the next paradigm. We did conclude that was where our solution resided. What followed was a process of in-depth personal and collective exploration over several months. The process involved learning the capacity of the human mind to tap into a superconsciousness beyond our own personal consciousness. We defined this ability as quantum-thinking. A significant part of the process was the in-depth discussions which involved validating, refining, and integrating our various experiences. The final solution looked nothing like our initial discussions of the present techniques and methodologies. This is an example of third-way thinking. We attribute our discovery of quantum-thinking to both our quest for group consensus and our willingness to go beyond the obvious in achieving a solution to producing the next-generation seminar in creativity and innovation.

♦ Systems Thinking [6]

The use of systems thinking is an excellent example of a new team competency for a synergistic team. The following example illustrates the application of this process using the foundation of empowerment principles discussed in chapter 4.

Responsibility: What new area of professional mastery could our team achieve to significantly enhance our synergistic performance? (What's the opportunity?)

Master systems thinking — for individual and team problem solving.

Empowerment: What new mindset, skills, and competencies must we learn in order to successfully master this new technique? (What/how are we going to do it?)

1) Read Peter Senge's book *The Fifth Discipline*.

2) Each team member writes a one-page summary of designated chapters and shares them with the team for questions, clarifications, and feedback.

3) Apply the systems thinking approach to a specific team problem or opportunity.

4) Practice, practice, and practice until systems thinking is mastered as a tool.

Accountability: In what ways could we hold ourselves *unquestionably* accountable for having mastered this technique? (How do we measure or evaluate what we committed to?)

1) Read two chapters per week. Since the book has 21 chapters, completion should occur in 10 weeks.

2) Allow for question-and-answer sessions among team members to ensure that everyone understands each chapter summary. Have team members grade each other.

3) Use the expanded systems picture to locate the activity of greatest leverage (locate the trim tab) for the problem or opportunity chosen.

4) Mastery occurs when the application of this skill solves the problem. See Figure 7.

Systems Thinking Example

Figure 7 illustrates a systems approach to dealing with an organization's drop in sales/market share.

Top Circle: Short-term (low-cost) obvious solution involves upgrading the marketing process and/or materials coupled with an expanded and a more forceful effort in sales.

Result: In some cases this approach does bring about a short-term increase in sales and market share. Eventually, sales drop again because the problem is more fundamental.

Delay: The "delay" indicates the time frame necessary to attempt the short-term solution (top circle) until the realization occurs that it will not solve the problem. At this point a shift to the lower circle occurs.

Lower Circle: The expanded systems approach, which involves the identification of the various dimensions of the business operation which impact sales, is much more inclusive and fundamental.

Business Unit Problem: Drop in Sales/Marketshare

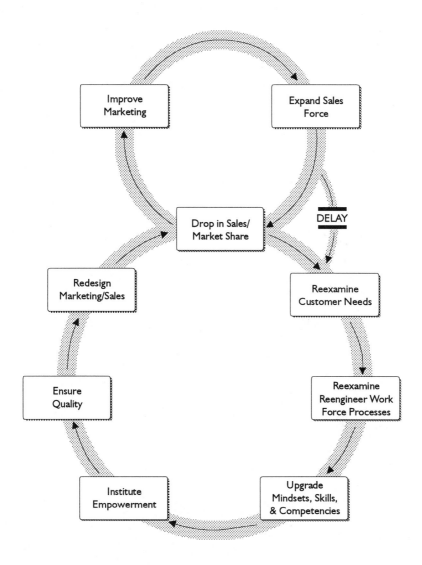

Figure 7.   Systems thinking diagram where the upper circle represents a short-term solution and the lower circle represents the long-term solution. The delay is the time frame for the upper circle solution to fail.

Guillory and Galindo

In systems thinking, the point of leverage (or the trim tab) is an activity in the lower circle which has the greatest impact in solving the problem. In this example, it is upgrading people skills. If this activity is effectively pursued, it affects all the other activities in the lower circle.

Part III.

Organizational Support System

A support system provides nurturing, resources, commitment, and an expectation of high performance.

The Authors

Chapter 10. **Organizational Support System**

♦ Introduction

Besides competent employees, an organizational support system is *the* most crucial component in successfully implementing an empowerment initiative. An organizational support system consists of the following major components:

1) Organizational Leadership

2) Management Commitment

3) Empowerment Infrastructure

The discussion of this part (Part III) of the text follows the flow diagram for the comprehensive implementation of empowerment shown on pages 218-20. In this chapter we will present an overview of each of the three components above as a prelude to their in-depth discussion in the following chapters.

♦ Organizational Leadership

Organizational leadership plays a pivotal role in instituting cultural transformation. Their process begins with acquiring the information and knowledge necessary to become committed to the empowerment initiative. An inherent part of becoming committed involves the personal process of creating an internally sourced empowerment vision, acquiring passion for the vision, and confirming the inner knowing that when the inevitable difficulties and setbacks occur, she or he will prevail. In instituting empowerment, adversity, setbacks, and continual uncertainty are certainties. The only question is, how do we prevail in spite of these obstacles?

For example, a common situation leadership experiences is employee resistance to greater accountability corresponding to greater delegated authority. Such situations provide a convenient excuse for leadership and management to return to hierarchical operation. The committed leader convinces managers and employees that hierarchy is not only unacceptable, but an unworkable alternative in today's competitive world. High-involvement, delegation, and accountability are all necessities for effectively operating in today's business environment, and are not negotiable.

In a similar manner, it is not uncommon for management to strongly resist not only their apparent loss of control, but their necessity to master new interpersonal management and team skills. The energy and persistence necessary to overcome these objections can be enormous. Again, aggressive, committed leadership must make it clear that the change process is not negotiable. Management anxiety and resistance are understandable, but will not prevent the necessity for empowerment.

The following example illustrates a common occurrence many organizations experience when implementing empowerment. That is, that a simple directive from the top will not produce visible results in terms of a transformed culture.

> When Gene began the empowerment initiative, he loved the idea. Finally, there was a way to get greater employee buy-in to business success. After one year, when he still heard complaints about managers and quality was no better, he called his vice presidents together and wanted an explanation. "We've all been through the empowerment training," one VP volunteered. "I guess we're not really sure what you want us to do." Gene sat stunned. He slowly and carefully chose his words. "Let me be clear. You are responsible and accountable for ensuring that you push decision making and problem solving to the lowest levels of the organization. People must be prepared for their new level of responsibility. This will be

a part of your performance review and tied to your bonus. What support do you need to be successful? We cannot go back if we are going to stay competitive."

The reality that Gene was experiencing is that empowerment is a long-term process and shows the least results in the first stage, which may be one or two years. He was also learning that the process will not succeed by a leadership directive to "go forth and empower your people." Leadership must play an active role in promoting the empowerment initiative and establishing a permanent support system.

Communication of Expectations Is Essential

In addition to active participation, leadership must understand that instituting empowerment is not an overnight process. They must clearly communicate the rationale for the new initiative and its value to the organization. This must be done *continually* in a sufficiently inviting and persuasive manner that it is accepted and embraced through self-enrollment by a critical segment of the work force. An essential part of this communication process involves the clear articulation of the organization's guiding principles. The guiding principles provide the framework for the reality of the new vision. It establishes concrete expectations of behaviors and performance. For example, the guiding principles for the Texas Instruments empowerment initiative are shown beginning on page 138.

GUIDING PRINCIPLES FOR AN EMPOWERED
TEAM-BASED ORGANIZATION
Defense Systems and Electronics Group (DSEG)

Principle 1:   We will create business strategies that provide opportunities for sustained competitive advantage and individual growth. Achieved through:

- Customer focus
- Continuous improvement (coupled with break-through improvement)
- People involvement

Principle 2:   Sustained breakthrough performance improvements will be achieved through work design/business process engineering advancements coupled with technological advancements.

Principle 3:   We will design our business processes to include only value-added activities that are required to meet customer expectations.

Principle 4:   Every Tler is responsible and accountable for achieving business objectives. Critical dimensions for ownership:

- Capability at the point of execution
- Information at the point of execution
- Decision making at the point of execution
- Recognition, rewards, and advancement tied to the effectiveness of both the decisions and the execution.

Principle 5:   We will foster a commitment to DSEG's objectives, values, and beliefs by creating an environment which aligns them with the individual Tler's objectives, values, and beliefs.

Principle 6: Continuous learning will form DSEG's foundation, enabling increased responsiveness, flexibility, and innovation.

Principle 7: We will reward and recognize TIers based on both achieving organizational (DSEG/Business Unit) expectations and demonstrating desired individual behaviors. Desired behaviors include:

- Empowering leadership
- Innovation and creativity
- Collaboration/teamwork
- Honesty and integrity
- Continuous learning

Principle 8: Our fundamental working relationship will be one of partnership where we share knowledge, information, responsibility, risk, and success. Partnering factors:

- Necessary capabilities
- Common objectives
- Interdependency
- Mutual trust
- Diverse perspectives

Principle 9: We will value diversity.

Principle 10: We will live by these guiding principles without exception.

In summary, it is leadership's role to *live* the vision and *model* the principles.

Guillory and Galindo

♦ **Management Commitment**

The role of management is to make it happen. This segment of the work force is literally caught in the middle of the change process. Most of these individuals have devoted years to being good citizens and contributing to the success of the organization and should be acknowledged for their contribution. However, with the incorporation of empowerment, they are now faced with a dramatic change in job security, roles and responsibilities, and status. In order to secure their commitment, it is vital that they be facilitated through this transition by education, training, and a shift in mindset in terms of their new roles.

The natural consequence of high employee involvement is a conscious or unconscious process of flattening the hierarchy. The more competently employees perform independently, the less necessity for managing. The less necessity for managing, the less meaningful is the boss-employee relationship. What emerges is a collegial relationship and the merging of multiple levels of the organization into fewer levels.

In many cases, employees are already sufficiently competent to assume expanded responsibilities for which they have not been granted authority. Such cases are the most traumatic for managers who have not continued to improve their own skills and competencies. Thus, job security becomes their major concern when conscious reduction of the hierarchy is a major implementation practice. This situation is quite different from one where highly competent, contributing managers and employees are downsized. We believe these situations are caused primarily by poor leadership planning in forecasting and anticipating the future.

Changing Roles and Responsibilities

Another factor faced by management is the significant change in roles and responsibilities. The new roles involve the following transitions:

1) Manager to facilitator

2) Controller to delegator of authority

3) Organizer to coordinator

4) Supervisor to coach

These changes require both a transformation in mindset *and* the mastery of new skills and competencies. Perhaps the more difficult of these is the transformation in mindset. There is a popular saying: "Change your mindset and you change your organization. Your organization is located between the ears of your employees."

A manager's mindset can be affected in two major ways. One is the loss in prestige which comes from no longer being a manager or a supervisor in the traditional status sense. Second is the loss of power, authority, and control which were traditionally synonymous with these titles. The truth is, earning a management position represents hard work and achievement, and should be acknowledged as such.

In empowered organizations, however, power, authority, and control are more associated with high performance than they are with position or title. Therefore, the transformation in mindset necessary is to adopt a way of thinking which views a valuable, influential employee as one who performs competently with the least amount of oversight or direction.

Cultural Transformation Requires a Rite of Passage

It is not unusual that most managers and employees will have to go through some form of the five-step "Death and Dying" process discussed by Elisabeth Kübler-Ross.[7]

1) Denial

2) Reaction

3) Bargaining

4) Guilt

5) Acceptance

Facilitating an individual, a team, or an organization through this process is an essential part of any cultural transformation. The essential elements in facilitating this process are:

1) Surfacing employees' beliefs which are the source of their fear of change.

2) Discussing and invalidating those beliefs which are self-limiting or have no basis in reality.

3) Convincing employees that they are significantly more capable and resilient to change than they realize.

If this process is bypassed by overemphasizing techniques, methodologies, and measurements, the change initiative will surely be unsuccessful. For example, numerous organizations have attempted quality, empowerment, and re-engineering initiatives with almost total emphasis on how to do it. Inevitably, the initiative stalls and is subsequently abandoned. The underestimated, and possibly most difficult, part of the change process is the shift in mindset from "I do what I'm told" to "I take the initiative to learn new skills and competencies in order to remain a value-added employee."

Managers who successfully navigate the five-step Kübler-Ross process become an organization's most valued resource in the empowerment transition because of two major reasons. First, we doubt that empowerment can successfully take hold on any permanent basis without significant management commitment. Second, managers and supervisors bring years of practical experience and know-how about how the system works and how things get done that can make the successful implementation of empowerment infinitely easier. Again, the key is to have managers and supervisors accept and commit to their new roles and responsibilities. The changing roles and responsibilities of managers will be discussed in more detail in chapter 12.

♦ Empowerment Infrastructure

Simply stated, without an empowerment infrastructure to oversee and support the process, the empowerment initiative will be unsuccessful. The sequence of actions discussed below correspond to the flow diagram beginning on page 218. Establishing an infrastructure begins with an oversight group, such as a task team or steering team. This group is usually representative of the entire organizational structure, particularly those segments crucial to the success of the initiative. It is usually coordinated by someone from the leadership ranks who reports directly to the CEO or president. An additional support senior executive, who may or may not be part of the team, is an empowerment champion. This is an individual who is passionately committed to empowerment. This individual must be able to devote 50 percent or more of her or his compensated time to this activity over several years. It is also necessary for members of the task team to have compensated time as they begin to play key roles in the implementation process throughout the organization. For example, most organizations have full-time empowerment facilitators to assist business units and teams with the implementation process. These are individuals who have gone through extensive training and have been taught critical facilitation skills.

Role of the Empowerment Task Team

After the task team goes through its own process of education and commitment, implementation usually begins with fact-finding, analysis, and some form of an organizational empowerment assessment. This assessment should provide an evaluation of individuals, teams, leadership, and the overall organization in terms of their readiness to initiate the empowerment process. The assessment should also serve as a baseline measurement (relative to future measurements) as well as to identify specific areas of weakness. For example, it is not unusual when beginning an empowerment initiative to discover that employees are more competent to perform independently than they have been allowed. Management and leadership interventions are usually the first areas for addressing this situation in terms of training, education, and commitment. Initial assessments also reveal that holding self and others accountable is the most common weakness in most organizations. Thus, preparatory education and training are essential to prevent initial accountability difficulties relating to breakdown in expectations.

At this point, the task team begins the process of formulating an empowerment plan. An essential part of this process is a planning session where the various functions of the empowerment infrastructure are clearly established. The culmination of the planning session, several weeks later, is the formulation of a detailed empowerment plan. In practice, most organizations begin training and implementation processes *before* they seriously consider a support infrastructure. Therefore, the *logical* sequence we have described is rarely followed and is not a necessity. What is vitally important to understand is that, at some point in the process, instituting an empowerment infrastructure will be necessary for success.

Now that we have briefly discussed the three major components of the organizational support system, we will explore the function of each of these in greater detail in the following chapters.

Chapter 11. **Role of Leadership**

♦ Introduction

We define leadership as the impetus which drives an organization in achieving its vision. Leadership is the driving force which transforms vision into reality. If the vision is challenging and ambitious, the corresponding level of leadership commitment will have to be equally great. In this chapter we discuss the role of leadership in terms of the following topics: leadership commitment, education and awareness, leadership practices and procedures, the new leadership, and leadership implementation strategies.

♦ Leadership Commitment

Committing to empowerment, or any of the transformational initiatives such as quality and diversity, can be difficult. The reason is we cannot really know the extent of our commitment until we encounter the inevitable difficulty of greatest challenge, and successfully overcome it. Commitment is discovered midstream when we are most challenged by the process. For example, when we discover, by experience, the investment of time and energy required to have employees perform in a self-accountable manner, it might appear easier to go back to a hierarchical way of operating. It is only after we discover that the initiation of empowerment to any significant extent is an irreversible process, do we come to the conclusion that the only question is *how* do we make it work.

In addition to the challenges of implementation, the loss of management control of information, power, and process can be equally traumatic. This reaction may be justified if an organization is proceeding on the assumption that empowerment means delegation. An executive *should* experience trauma if, in fact, employees are being granted authority without ensuring:

1) Delegation at the level of an employee's ability to perform (or just beyond).

2) Clearly defined responsibilities and accountability within specific guidelines.

3) Availability of organizational support when needed.

On the other hand, the traditional sources of leadership power are exactly the ones which need to be shared — information, decision making, and control — in order for empowerment to work. This can be a challenging process for all levels of leadership.

Commitment Requires More Than Business Rationale

The level of commitment required of leadership is greater than that required of management and the work force since leadership has the power to stop or sustain the initiative. In most cases, commitment solely from a business perspective will probably not be sufficient to successfully carry the process to completion unless survival is threatened. The high degree of personal and organizational transformation required will naturally generate a high level of resistance and perhaps even unconscious sabotage — particularly in organizations which are relatively healthy and profitable and do not *have* to change in the short term.

For example, a common tactic used by employees who resist change is simply to ignore it. They willingly go through any training and planning required and then proceed to ignore implementation. The thought which commonly runs through this employee's mind is, "I'll know they are serious if they are still singing the same song a year from now and someone steps in to hold me accountable." This is why leadership has to be committed from a driving force which goes beyond business motivation.

148

The driving force which often inspires passionate commitment is a personal vision of service. The source of this vision is an internal desire to create an environment where people can maximize their ability to perform. Such a commitment must be sustained over several years before permanent change begins to occur. An example of this type of leadership, proposed by Robert K. Greenleaf, is Servant-Leadership.[8] According to Robert Greenleaf, "A servant-leader is a person who begins with a natural feeling of wanting to serve *first* — to help, support, encourage, and lift up others. And because of their noble role model, others begin to lead by serving."

A Dallas, Texas-based organization which espouses these values in its everyday functioning is TDIndustries. Led by Jack Lowe, Jr., the CEO, TDIndustries embraces and aspires to operate according to the philosophy of Robert Greenleaf. When TDIndustries decided to seriously implement their diversity initiative, the *first* statement was, "it is right!" By the way, TDIndustries is a construction company that has been cited as one of the nation's top 100 employers to work for by the publication, *The 100 Best Companies to Work for in America.* They were also selected in 1995 as Commercial Contractor of the Year by *Contracting Business* magazine.

The sequential processes of committing to an empowerment initiative are the following: becoming knowledgeable of the business necessities; acquiring a comprehensive understanding of empowerment, and having an in-depth experience of the challenges involved. This sequence follows the outline on page 218 and is discussed in the following section.

◆ Education and Awareness

One of the major roles of leadership is to be knowledgeable of major changes occurring in business management operation. Aside from the competitive advantages inherent in high-involvement, the four necessities we discussed earlier — *quality, customization, speed,* and *service* — require high-involvement simply to survive. A critical part of the education process is to discover how these four necessities relate to your particular organization or business operation. For example, a central theme in the implementation of quality is having more employee contact with the customer. In order to operate effectively in this capacity, employees must learn skills formerly reserved for managers and salespeople. They must learn how to ask relevant questions and, most of all, learn how to listen to what a customer *needs*, so that these needs can be anticipated. The knowledge and training necessary to perform in this expanded capacity are essential ingredients of an empowered employee.

In addition to understanding the business reasons driving empowerment, leadership must be exposed to a comprehensive understanding of an empowerment program (page 218). This process involves understanding the possible challenges, consequences, and opportunities — both within the framework of business necessities and the increasing desire of employees to have greater ownership of their work. As organizations streamline for high performance, they simultaneously retain those employees who require the least amount of supervision and direction. It would be counterproductive and outdated to retain a high degree of hierarchy and structure — and ultimately unworkable with such employees.

The final step in the process of committing to empowerment is exposure to an *in-depth experience* of the challenges of empowerment. These are sharing power, giving up control, rewarding performance, reducing hierarchy, and transforming one's own fundamental personal beliefs. An effective seminar or workshop should include these elements, in addition to education. After commitment is established, there should be ongoing education and training involving implementation strategies and skills building consistent with the new philosophy. Empowerment, by its very nature, is a continuous-learning process for *everyone*.

Having this in-depth exposure to empowerment provides the basis for the initial stage of an organizational (leadership) commitment. The second stage commitment to such an initiative occurs when leadership endorses a comprehensive plan with measurable objectives and allocates the financial support necessary to implement the plan. Once commitment is established, the role of leadership is to be living examples of the empowerment initiative, as discussed in the following section.

♦ Leadership Practices and Procedures

The rule for credible leadership is to *live* the vision and *model* the values. Living the vision involves adopting a mindset that the vision is already a reality. It literally exists, at present, within the minds of leadership. Their everyday example in the workplace, in turn, creates this expectation in others, and ultimately creates the reality. Leaders essentially project themselves into the vision and literally *pull* the organization into that future reality.

This process takes form by establishing both personal and business objectives and goals. It also involves setting the direction of business units consistent with the organization's vision and goals through written and verbal communications, being the head cheerleader, and modeling high-involvement behavior. The following example illustrates how the leadership of Texas Instruments served as a model to the organization in emphasizing its commitment to high-involvement.

In its attempt to communicate the importance of teamwork to the organization, Texas Instruments reorganized its traditional leadership structure into a leadership team structure. The new structure is a circle of eight critical business functions with a core leadership team of three executives. The core team is titled the Office of the Chief Executive. This reorganization provides the opportunity for broad input and consensus, participative decision making, and cross-functional teaming at the executive level.

Modeling the values is being a living example of the expectations of others in terms of behavior. However, it should be acknowledged that leaders are also in a continuing growth process and may violate the values on occasion, just as other employees do. This might occur when there are strong pressures to achieve business objectives and goals, no matter what needs to be done. Situations where values, morals, and ethics have to be reconciled with business necessities are "moments of truth." They provide the opportunity for ethical breakthroughs. Ethical breakthroughs commonly occur in indeterminate situations. In such situations, e.g., downsizing, environmental concerns, societal impact, etc., decisions are made by judgment rather than solely on the basis of information and analysis. Judgment is based upon an organization's vision, mission, principles, and values, and ultimately upon an individual's morals and ethics.

Finally, it is leadership's responsibility to continually anticipate the future. In other words, leadership is responsible for overseeing, evolving, and, when necessary, transforming the culture as a function of the changing business environment. The ability of leadership to adapt to rapid change is described by the five-stage model outlined in the following section.

Levels of Leadership

One way to model the various levels of leadership as a function of changing business conditions is shown by the descriptions in Table 2. This table describes the level of responsible leadership as a function of five existing organizational conditions resulting from the external business environment. Each of these five stages — vision, awareness, urgency, breakdown, and crisis — is discussed below.

Vision

Most organizations do not suffer from a lack of leadership's ability to define the future — that is, the creation of a vision which *anticipates* their market's needs and wants. The greater challenge is convincing a *comfortable* work force to change when it is not necessary. Some organizational leaders have come to the conclusion (by inaction) that it is simply not possible to achieve widespread fundamental change without some degree of urgency. That is, visionary change in anticipation of the future is simply not practical, or even possible. Some leaders in this situation have learned how to *create* urgency, in spite of the predictable upheaval the organization experiences. In any case, it would appear that visionary change, although most desirable, requires a leader who is sufficiently convincing, forceful, clear, and able to capture the imagination and trust of a critical part of the work force. Probably the most important characteristic is the courage to act in spite of expected resistance.

Awareness

The next motivation for change is *awareness* of the changing business environment, coupled to customer demands and wants. Inherent in this awareness are the first signs of

Table 2. Stages of Change as a Function of Responsible Leadership.

Stage	Description	Condition	
Vision	The anticipation of change or customer's demands, wants, and needs.	Financially healthy, on the leading edge of change.	**High**
Awareness	The recognition of the need for change or customer demands and wants.	Financially healthy, responsive, tuned to the winds of change.	Responsible Leadership
Urgency	The necessity to respond to change or customer demands.	Financially hurting, downsizing, pretending to accept change.	
Breakdown	The unwillingness to adequately respond to change or customer demands.	Financially in trouble, downsizing, pretending to accept change.	
Crisis	The final stages of existence in presently existing form.	Financially bankrupt.	**Low**

declining revenues, which are not rectified by continuous improvement processes, policies, or procedures. Most competently led organizations take action at this stage, whether it is something serious in terms of commitment or an initial awareness process. However, many organizations in this stage tend to resist the changing reality and require more *visibly experienced* pain as a motivation for serious change. What they require is a state of urgency.

Urgency

Not to worry, more visibly experienced pain is on the way — usually quicker than anticipated. This is *urgency*. Urgency is analogous to treading water. The major reasons for the retention of a customer base are usually a one-of-a-kind item (sole source), long-term loyal customers whose patience is wearing thin, or hard core selling. This organization attempts to remain financially solvent by downsizing. Oddly enough, many organizations in this stage initiate superficial programs which pretend to want the fundamental change necessary. For many organizations, with average leadership, the pain (loss in revenue) is sufficient to take a stand for change — and many begin to do so. The problem is time. Can the organization be turned around before *breakdown* sets in?

Breakdown

Breakdown is analogous to going under and resurfacing in an attempt to avoid drowning. Everyone gets the message by now. Downsizing, continuous improvement, and all the obvious measures have not stemmed the tide of decline. It is difficult, if not impossible, to *save* the organization in its present form at this point. The true acknowledgment of resistance is openly discussed and two alternatives exist.

Guillory and Galindo

One, get a new CEO from outside with *carte blanche* power to do whatever is necessary to save the organization. Two, continue in denial to the stage of crisis. Even if the first alternative is chosen, there is no assurance that crisis will not occur.

Crisis

The final stage of the conditional change process is almost totally forced by external circumstances. This is crisis. Crisis is the final stage where there are no choices remaining. The organization either goes out of business or is radically redesigned in a format which attempts to be responsive to the new reality. Many, if not most, of the former employees (who resisted change) are no longer with the organization. In essence, a new organization is born with revolutionary leadership (relative to the previous leaders).

Tapping Human Consciousness

The reason it is so difficult to be a visionary leader is that most leaders have not developed the ability to tap into the winds of change driven by human consciousness. The ability to tap into human consciousness is in direct proportion to one's own self-mastery through conscious personal growth. This is not intellectual knowledge acquired from academic study, but a deeply personal transformational process. Not many individuals, let alone leaders, consciously embark on such a journey. However, the number is increasing dramatically. These are leaders that we refer to as "the new leadership."

156

♦ The New Leadership — The Future Is Now

In the present knowledge-based era, success is in direct proportion to employee competence and well-being. This reality has caused organizations to become more people-focused in terms of employee quality of life. Employee quality of life is the *experience* of being fully valued, included, and provided the opportunity for full self-expression in terms of one's capabilities and talents.[9] As leading organizations have become more people-focused, a new dimension of leadership has simultaneously emerged. That dimension involves doing what is ethically, morally, and socially right, even when it is not a business imperative. For example, visionary CEOs who realize that diversity is inevitable, need not be forced to aggressively implement diversity because of provable business necessities. They *lead* from a spiritually-sourced motivation of commitment to total employee inclusion *in addition to* responsibly managing the health of the business. The two are not incompatible!

Spiritually-Sourced Leadership

Spirituality is the domain of consciousness which transcends the human mind. It is a domain of wisdom. It is characterized by harmony, interconnectedness, and oneness. Gaining access to this domain of wisdom requires the setting aside of one's present way of thinking in order to experience an expanded understanding of how we might work together in more mutually contributing ways. Such an experience has the power to reshape one's moral and ethical values. The truly visionary leaders of today are driven by this source of wisdom in the way they conduct the operation of their organizations. An example of a spiritually-sourced code of ethics is the following:

1) Treat others with dignity, respect, and love.

2) View human equality as a context for ethical behavior.

3) Realize that everything that exists is interdependent and interconnected — nature, animals, and humans.

4) View our organization, community, country, and world as one.

When this type of code of ethics becomes a reality, an organization experiences a profound shift in consciousness. This shift is reflected as a paradigm shift in performance, profitability, and employee growth and well-being.

Spiritually-sourced leadership is also reflected in organizations which are committed to preserving the environment and protecting consumers without the necessity for exhaustive scientific proof of the dangers of their products. In the long (and sometimes short) run, all of these nonhard-line issues can result in very dire consequences for businesses, consumers, and the environment. Given the interconnected nature of the world today and the accelerated rate of events, the necessity for spiritually-sourced leadership is urgent. It will become an absolute requirement for twenty-first century leadership.

Those business leaders who view themselves as an integral part of their community also assume a moral obligation to the community's overall welfare. They do not view this obligation as solely philanthropic, but a natural part of the connectedness of the human condition. Recognizing how separation and polarization can adversely affect the health of a community, the business leadership of Dallas, Texas, created a progressive diversity covenant. This agreement came about after several years of challenging dialogue by a diverse group of business leaders called the Dallas Together Forum. It is a perfect example of the recognition of the interconnectedness between business and the community by a group of visionary leaders.

> In 1991, the business leaders of Dallas, Texas, initiated a challenging process for more effectively including ethnic minorities into the mainstream of Dallas business. The result was the creation of the Dallas Together Covenant for Workplace Diversity and Minority Business Opportunity. The Covenant, a *first-of-its-kind program*, is designed to improve economic opportunities for ethnic minorities. The Covenant has been signed by more than 200 businesses in the Dallas area. It involves publicly stating and subsequently reporting, on an annual basis, minority business commitment in terms of:
>
> 1) The dollar amount of purchases from minority-owned businesses
> 2) The ethnic-minority percentages of new hires
> 3) The ethnic-minority percentages of newly filled professional, management, and board positions.

♦ Leadership Implementation Strategies

The following items are a checklist of those empowerment implementation strategies that leadership is ultimately responsible and accountable for ensuring. Although some of these may overlap with the activities of the empowerment champion and the empowerment task force, leadership has the ultimate responsibility to ensure their effective implementation.

1) Create an empowerment vision.

2) Establish empowerment objectives and goals.

3) Establish management expectations and accountability.

4) Provide empowerment education and training for the entire organization.

5) Establish an empowerment task force.

6) Select an empowerment champion.

7) Confirm and support a comprehensive empowerment plan.

8) Ensure ongoing executive leadership education and training in empowerment.

9) Reduce unnecessary levels of management as a function of expanded organizational empowerment.

10) Ensure an empowerment infrastructure.

11) Encourage and provide employees with greater information, knowledge, power, and rewards.

12) Acknowledge and reward empowerment successes.

13) Create a climate for a learning organization.

The process of getting these items done involves the commitment and cooperation of management. We now turn our attention to the radically changing roles and responsibilities necessary to manage empowerment.

Chapter 12. **Managing Empowerment**

♦ Introduction

As we have stated previously, the role of management is to make it happen. Making it happen requires commitment. Commitment does not occur as a result of a directive from upper management or leadership. It occurs through education, training, and the opportunity for managers to confront and invalidate the fears they experience as a result of the change process. An important part of the education process is the realization that high employee involvement is a competitive necessity about which we have no choice. Once this reality has set in, we can seriously begin the implementation process.

Managing the implementation of empowerment requires the ability to competently perform an essential set of management skills. These skills are described in the discussion of the following topics:

1) Delegation

2) Coaching

3) Changing roles and responsibilities of managers

4) Guidelines for facilitating employee empowerment

Although this list is not exhaustive, it does include the crucial functions that managers are immediately faced with when implementing empowerment. These four topics comprise the discussion of this chapter.

◆ Delegation

Delegation is the act of granting authority to an individual or a team to perform a task for which he, she, or they will be held accountable for the results produced. Responsible delegation is delegating within an individual's or a team's capability or slightly beyond.

In the dictionary the word *empower* is defined as "delegation with authority." When applied to the *practice* of managing empowerment, confusion arises when a task is delegated to someone who does not have the capability to accomplish the assignment. Can you truly *empower* someone to do something for which he or she is not capable? The answer, of course, is "no." For this reason, we make a clear distinction between personal empowerment and delegation, as they apply to the workplace.

Personal empowerment is an internally-derived capacity to perform, while delegation is the act of being granted authority to demonstrate that capability. Therefore, a manager cannot personally empower an employee or a co-worker simply by granting authority to perform a task. Within the framework of these distinctions, responsible delegation with authority is an operational necessity for empowerment to work.

The reason this distinction is so vital to understand is because the corresponding expectation involved in responsible delegation is accountability — of both managers and employees. Accountability is the willingness to answer for the results produced from an assignment for which one is given authority. When a task is delegated, it is either within or beyond the capability of the one assigned the task. This is where managerial judgment becomes crucial. When an assignment is clearly within one's capability, success normally follows, although little or no growth occurs in terms of expanded personal empowerment. Managerial judgment is the ability to distinguish situations in which one's personal beliefs and attitudes might influence the underutilization of personnel from situations involving individuals who are clearly unwilling to grow.

The following scenario describes a manager struggling with the issue of control. He is forced to resolve the issue because of the changing complexity of work processes. Such situations are not uncommon when implementing high-involvement initiatives.

As the deadline grew closer for certification review, Joe knew it was going to be close. He had brought people through this process several times before in various companies where he had worked and he knew how to do it. Meeting the deadline was Joe's excuse for going into a "command and control" mode to make it happen.

In his review, he was criticized by subordinates for a lack of coaching and his unavailability. "Who has time?" Joe thought, but he knew that wasn't the issue. Just because he had done it several times before didn't mean it was done the best, most efficient way. He decided to reexamine his process and bring subordinates into the decision making about time schedules up front. "Mostly, I don't trust these people. That's why I don't delegate," he confided to a facilitator. "But it's getting too complicated to do it alone. It's hard to spend time to get to know my people when all I think is needed is to get the job done! I'm still working on really seeing that people are our most important resource. I have to spend time developing their capabilities or we'll be running in place."

When an assignment is delegated which is beyond the demonstrated capability of an employee or co-worker, coaching is an *inseparable* part of that assignment. A manager or supervisor is obliged to conscientiously assist the empowered growth of that employee *in addition* to ensuring the successful accomplishment of the task. Within the framework of these distinctions, responsible delegation of authority is an operational necessity for an empowered organization.

◆ Coaching

Coaching is an interactive process, either in pairs or as a team, of facilitating the enhancement of an individual's ability to perform by successfully accomplishing a challenging, previously unachieved task. The result of coaching is the acquisition of new skills, knowledge, and an expanded mindset of self-competence. Coaching is fun, yet difficult at times, because it requires the development of interpersonal skills. To know and to tell someone *how* to do something is not difficult. To influence them to risk beyond their comfort zone to acquire expanded capability requires trust. Trust usually results from the process of establishing in-depth interpersonal relationship and communication. A manager is responsible for initiating the interpersonal interaction and openness that leads to the mutual level of trust required.

These issues naturally arise as an integral part of the teaming process, particularly where a great deal of self-direction is desired. They are even further exacerbated where teams are cross-functional or diverse. Teams must set aside the time and commitment necessary to resolve whatever unique issues they identify in order to effectively serve internal and external customers. This process involves a combination of overcoming and releasing mutual stereotypical beliefs and attitudes and ethnocentric values, and laying the foundation for a team (or organizational) value system based upon mutual trust, respect, and equality. Such a foundation establishes the basis for the most effective utilization of empowerment as a management style.

♦ Changing Roles and Responsibilities of Managers

The changing roles of managers continue to be a challenge for organizations attempting to become more empowered. The following discussion is a summarization of seven skills we view as vital for managing employees towards high performance. The seven management skills are: evaluating, planning, organizing, decision making, motivating, developing, and leading.[10]

1) Evaluating

Evaluating involves determining what needs to be done in order to increase quality, productivity, and the growth and well-being of employees. Evaluation usually implies a comparison of the present status with an established goal or sequence of accomplishments leading to an established goal. If neither of these exists, such an evaluation may lead to the realization that the team, unit, or organization is not totally clear as to specifics of what is to be accomplished. "Hazy goals produce hazy results." When an evaluation indicates that established goals are not being accomplished, it raises the question of what should be done differently *and* how people have to change for these different procedures to really matter. When an evaluation indicates the successful accomplishment of an established goal, then a team, unit, or an organization is in the enviable position of being content or setting higher standards for themselves and possibly the market. In all three situations, the question is, what do we do about our present situation?

For example, if the real estate market is soft; that is, houses are not selling in normal quantities and prices are falling, what should we do as an independent office? During difficult times, an organization discovers who is truly committed, and to what extent, to the organization's success. It is easy to be involved during good times, but the test usually comes when times are tough. Therefore, what to do may begin with reassessing individual commitment and making whatever mutually appropriate adjustments are necessary. Evaluating may involve going back to basics and redefining such questions as: What specifically do we do or sell? Who specifically is our customer? Are we serving them better than anyone competing? What do we need to be doing differently and innovatively to meet the present challenge? When questions such as these are clarified, the answers naturally lead to *how* we need to change our situation to achieve success.

2) **Planning**

Planning involves determining what needs to be done to achieve increased productivity and profit while maintaining the growth and well-being of employees. After answering the back-to-basics questions above and reassessing the ranks for commitment, the next management *coordinating* responsibility is establishing, interdependently, *what you are going for*. What is the goal that begins to define, retrospectively, the stepwise plan for success? Based upon the increased desire for productivity and profit, both systems improvement *and* people development will be required. According to the empowerment philosophy, the more employees embrace personal empowerment, the more receptive they are to procedures which ensure increased growth and productivity — and profit naturally follows. It is important that the team, unit, or organization is intimately involved in planning so that their ownership of the process is unquestionably established.

For example, if the plan is to significantly increase the quality of a product or service, the team, unit, or organization will have to accept training as an *integral part* of the process, rather than as an annoyance that takes them away from real work. It is vital that they come to realize that continuous learning provides the framework for understanding what they are attempting to change. Effective training not only involves a change in process, but a transformation in their fundamental way of thinking about performing a task. A vital component in planning is establishing that continuous learning is important in achieving quality.

3) **Organizing**

Organizing involves the coordination of the total unit's human, financial, and physical resources such that productivity, profit, and employee well-being are realized. Even though this is a management responsibility, and she or he will be held accountable, it is important that the team, unit, or organization also be involved in this process. The empowered manager's preoccupation is, how do we organize our activities in such a way that everyone's talent is maximized? And as a corollary, how do we ensure the opportunity for expanded personal empowerment and the elimination of personal and professional barriers?

For example, an empowered manager may organize her unit's tasks in such a manner that she sets the parameters, limitations, and to some extent the organizationally imposed guidelines. Then she requests the unit to establish the procedure for most effectively accomplishing the objective. It is vital in implementing this management style that employees have as much responsibility as possible, *with accountability*. This point is perhaps best summarized by a command attributed to General George Patton, "It's amazing how creative your people will become if you tell them where to be at what time, and don't tell them how to get there."

4) Decision making

Decision making involves addressing difficulties, problems, or new challenges encountered with the major focus for solutions on those directly involved. Decision making that involves processes or procedures is relatively straightforward and is usually best done by those directly involved. In a like manner, decisions involving policy and explicit procedure typically have straightforward guidelines. Making decisions about the performance of employees is a more difficult management skill. This is a responsibility which requires managerial maturity, not only in making a decision but carrying it out in a professional and compassionate manner. The basic rule is that you cannot effectively manage in others what you have not mastered in yourself. Holding others accountable for their performance is by far the most difficult skill which is necessary for the systematic incorporation of empowerment.

The determining characteristic of successful companies in the 1990s will be flexible decision making based upon a shared strategic vision. This means delegating decision-making powers to middle and line managers, with the simultaneous elimination of unnecessary management layers which stifle self-directed operation. A basic rule of human nature is that commitment to and ownership of a decision is synonymous with participation in the process. For example, many of the decisions involving quality customer service result from the direct interaction of line managers and workers with the customer, without the necessity of upper management's involvement.

5) Motivating

Motivating involves encouraging employees to perform to their maximum potential in an activity for which they are personally skilled and interested, confident of management's support and modeling. This is a critical function in a market where organizations will be requiring greater productivity from fewer employees. Rather than giving orders, managers will have to become skilled at motivating, advising, and facilitating. The benefits that come from the successful encouragement of employees to reach their maximum potential will be realized continuously with every project. High-performing employees add more to the bottom line of an organization's profit than any other single factor. Empowered, and therefore motivated, employees operate continuously in this manner.

6) Developing

Developing involves a concerted process of personal and professional growth of self and employees. The key here is to have employees realize that personal growth drives expanded empowerment and that professional development allows expanded creative expression of their newly acquired skills. Since quality is a market-driven necessity, new creative products and services are required to remain competitive. Therefore, continuous development is a customer-driven necessity. Development occurs most effectively where managers encourage training, interactive mentoring, and professional growth opportunities. In addition, they create an environment where development is not only valued, but is expected and correspondingly rewarded. This is another area where empowered managers lead by example.

7) Leading

Leading involves being a *living example* of the expectations of employees and therefore credibly inspiring exceptional individual and team performance. Leadership is a progressively participative process as a team, unit, or organization becomes more empowered. Therefore, leadership involves making certain that everyone understands and is committed to the established objectives and goals. It also involves continually providing the spark that drives the team, unit, or organization to success. The power of leadership in empowered organizations is sourced from a compelling, shared vision.

♦ Guidelines for Facilitating the Empowerment of an Employee or a Co-Worker

1) *Clearly explain and describe personal empowerment.*

Begin with a clear explanation of personal empowerment and a description of an empowered employee. Explain the relationship between personal responsibility, accountability, and empowerment.

An empowered employee is an individual who has the skills and the capability to solve expected and unexpected problems that arise from an assigned task, with the least amount of guidance and supervision. When guidance and supervision are necessary, they involve new learning in capability, and should not have to be a repeated lesson; although reinforcement may be necessary.

2) *Clearly explain and describe the job or task responsibilities and expectations.*

Provide a clearly explained (and written, where necessary) description of the job or task responsibilities and expectations of an employee until he or she clearly understands what the job or task entails and what is expected.

3) *Clearly present alternative resolutions to unmet responsibilities and expectations.*

Where necessary or appropriate, clearly explain or write what the recommendations will be if the job or task responsibilities and expectations are not met within a given time frame.

4) *Allow ample opportunity to make a decision.*

Allow the employee ample opportunity to decide if he or she is willing to assume the assigned task, given the requirements you have outlined. Make certain the employee is fully confident he or she has your support and is aware that his or her success is the same as your success.

5) *Secure employee ownership of the job or task.*

Provide an opportunity for employee input and feedback relative to the job or task responsibilities, expectations, and evaluation measures *before* proceeding to be certain that he or she claims personal ownership of the assignment.

Do not proceed to initiate a project unless there is a clear or reasonable level of ownership by the employee.

6) *Determine an appropriate job or task which facilitates employee development.*

It is the manager's responsibility to assign a job or task that is within or slightly exceeds the capability of the employee. This requires managerial mastery, which is an ongoing process.

7) *Establish specific time frames and provide honest feedback.*

As the employee proceeds to accomplish the project, establish specific time frames for progress reports, feedback, mentorship, and evaluation.

Discuss candidly whether the progress, quality, or the performance is meeting expectations established at the beginning of the project.

8) *Encourage employee personal and professional development.*

Recommend (or in necessary cases, strongly recommend) that the employee take personal or professional training in order to perform at the level of the assigned task.

Where resistance to personal or professional development is experienced, explain to the employee the relationship between expanded empowerment to perform and self-limitations, the professional benefits to be derived, and the practical value of personal growth in his or her everyday life.

9) *Where quality of performance does not meet responsibilities and expectations, act as specified in Guideline 3.*

Where the employee refuses to professionally develop to meet the expectations of the job or assigned task, the manager has one of two options:

a) Assign jobs or tasks which are only within the capability of the employee to perform in an empowered way.

b) Where appropriate indicate that, in the long run, their present capability to perform may not be sufficient for retention in that position. Therefore, transfer, reassignment, etc. may be necessary.

10) *Ultimately, develop a cooperative commitment to personal and organizational empowerment.*

The essence of operating in an empowered manner is that the choice to personally or professionally develop to meet job expectations is always with the employee, interdependently with a *committed* managerial and organizational support system.

Summary

Empowerment, as a way of managing, occurs by:

- Holding others accountable while simultaneously being responsible.

- Assuming employees can think and do for themselves, and allowing the struggles and mistakes that employees have to go through to *realize* they possess expanded capability.

- Treating employees as fully capable and able, and demonstrating an unwillingness to accept them as disempowered and victimized. This must be done with understanding and compassion.

- Coaching, but not taking away the personal responsibility of an employee.

- Mentoring the personal and professional development of employees.

- Ultimately, being an example of that which is required of employees. Employees are measurably more influenced by what a manager does than by what a manager says.

Now that we have established two of the three major components of an organizational support system — leadership and management — we will discuss the component which propels and sustains the process over time — the empowerment infrastructure.

Chapter 13. **Empowerment Infrastructure**

◆ Introduction

The empowerment infrastructure is the support system which ensures the successful implementation of empowerment. It consists of the internal structure, strategies, and processes necessary to sustain the initiative after an empowerment plan has been approved by leadership. The process of creating an infrastructure also involves the identification of key individuals and the roles they play in implementation. This chapter is a presentation and discussion of the major elements of an empowerment infrastructure as shown by the flow diagram on page 219: infrastructure task teams; designing a high-involvement organization; a high-involvement systems exercise; and integrated infrastructures.

◆ Infrastructure Task Teams

Creating an empowerment infrastructure usually begins by defining essential structures, guidelines, and functions to be performed by task teams. The work of the task teams should be an integrated part of other related initiatives, such as Teamwork; Quality; Reengineering; Environment, Safety & Health (ES&H); etc. Particularly, where the intent is to achieve a high-performance organization. The responsibilities of the various task teams are discussed as follows:

1) **Empowerment Business Impact** — The establishment of:

   i) Sound business reasons for empowerment, which are related to the bottom line from a financial standpoint.

ii) The relationship of empowerment to Quality, Teamwork, Reengineering, and ES&H, and other related initiatives.

iii) The relationship of empowerment to the organization's vision, mission, values, objectives, and strategic plan.

2) **Empowerment Leadership** — The establishment of:

i) An empowerment vision statement.

ii) Principles of empowerment.

iii) A set of clearly defined empowerment objectives (and timetables) which follows from the vision.

iv) Approval and support of an empowerment plan.

3) **Empowerment Organizational Structure and Roles** — The establishment of:

i) An organizational network for *making empowerment happen,* primarily using key positions of the existing organizational structure and human resources.

ii) Key individuals who oversee the coaching and implementation of empowerment, i.e., trainers, coordinators, coaches, strategists, and consultants.

iii) The roles and responsibilities of these key individuals.

4) **Guidelines for Organizational Levels** — The establishment of specific responsibilities and behaviors expected of:

  i) Senior leadership

  ii) Upper management

  iii) Middle management

  iv) First-line management/supervisors

  v) The broad-based work force

5) **Empowerment Communications Network** — The establishment of:

  i) A comprehensive *network* for the publication and dissemination of all information relating to the empowerment initiative.

  ii) A system and vehicles (publications, speeches, seminars, etc.) for the continuing communication of the organization's commitment to empowerment until it is achieved.

6) **Empowerment Accountability** — The establishment of:

  i) What management and employees should be accountable for in the area of empowerment.

  ii) How they will be held accountable through evaluations, measurements, metrics, etc.

  iii) What consequences there should be, if any, if mutually agreed-upon objectives are not achieved.

7) **Empowerment Plan** — The establishment of a comprehensive plan for achieving empowerment, which is confirmed by senior leadership, if one has not been established at the completion of the first phase.

The responsibilities of the infrastructure task teams are usually initiated as a one- or two-day working session. The participants include members of the empowerment task force as well as key managers and employees crucial to the implementation and success of the empowerment initiative. This working session may also include customers, suppliers, and internal and external consultants.

A subgroup of these participants (and any other important managers or employees) is selected to summarize the work of the task teams and create a comprehensive empowerment plan, including goals, timetables, and human and financial resources necessary for success. This plan is submitted to senior leadership for confirmation and implementation. At this point, the infrastructure task teams are disbanded and the plan for implementation is overseen by the empowerment task force.

◆ Designing a High-Involvement Organization

In order to perform the responsibilities of the various task teams, it is necessary for the participants to become knowledgeable about high-involvement practices. Although an in-depth understanding can be acquired from sources listed in the bibliography on page 233, particularly reference 11, the major components are summarized in the following discussion.

A high-involvement organization is one in which employee empowerment is central to its total operation. Individually and collectively, employees are primarily responsible and accountable for self-management, quality, continuous quality improvement, and controlling the production of a whole aspect of goods, products, or services.

High-involvement is consistent with some of the most cherished U. S. American values, such as *personal freedom, individualism, equality, human rights, competition, innovation,* and *entrepreneurship.* Making high-involvement work most effectively will require the balancing of personal freedom and individualism with *diversity, teamwork, obligation to others,* and *loyalty* to organization, society, and country; for global organizations, it will require an overriding commitment to the overall welfare of the world community.

Is High-Involvement the Right Choice?

Transition from the information paradigm to the present knowledge-based paradigm unquestionably confirms that a highly competent and continuously learning work force is an absolute necessity for competing in a global economy. High-involvement is best suited for organizations that provide goods, products, and services which require complex and continually changing processes. Examples include organizations involved in high technology, information systems, science and technology, engineering, electronics, and consumer products. It is also required for work forces that are highly skilled and required to make continuous decisions regarding internal processes and customers, such as banking, retail, consulting, hospitality, travel, education, health care, engineering, and construction.

The extent of high-involvement is directly proportional to the extent the work force has demonstrated, by performance or potential, the ability to meet or exceed customer expectations using self-management. High-involvement is a necessity for organizations that expect or require organization-wide innovation, individual and group-focused quality, fast response to problems and customer needs, continuous quality improvement, and a committed, stable work force.

Creating a High-Involvement Structure

In general, high-involvement flourishes in flattened, decentralized structures. Hierarchical, control-oriented structures tend to discourage, if not totally prohibit, high-involvement. One of the major objectives of a high-involvement system is to increase the *span of control*; that is, progressively increase the number of employees reporting to a manager or supervisor. For empowered organizations, this number may be as low as 10 or as high as 100 or greater. This is accomplished by the extensive establishment of teams, both temporary and permanent.

Key elements which influence the effectiveness of high-involvement, flattened structures are:[11]

- *Information* regarding the total operation of the organization,

- *Knowledge* of one's job and the organizational operation as a necessity for competent decision making,

- *Power* to carry out independent *and* interdependent decisions,

- *Rewards* which are tied to business success and performance, and are consistent with an employee's value system.

The organizational structure is like the basic architecture within which the work force functions and is typically represented by an organizational chart. High-involvement is fostered when the organization is centered around customers, products and services, (or a combination of these), rather than being structured by function, which inevitably forces hierarchy, since all functions merge at the top.

For large organizations, this is accomplished by the establishment of several or many autonomous small business units, i.e., SBUs, which produce a particular product or serve a particular group of customers. Where integration of small business units is a key factor, there may be a need for cross-functional work teams.

It is emphasized that the transition from management-orientation to high-involvement orientation should be gradual and progressively proactive. The rate should be determined by the extent of individual, team, and organizational empowerment along the continuum shown in Figure 1 (page 8).

Work Design

Work design in high-involvement organizations centers around the extensive expansion of two basic concepts: *individual job enrichment* and *work teams*. Both of these concepts involve greater employee information, knowledge, power, and rewards. They also involve greater employee *horizontal* and *vertical job expansion* and control. Horizontal job expansion refers to greater responsibility for the number of steps in producing a whole product or service. Vertical job expansion refers to greater responsibility for decision making regarding the work process of a whole product or service.

Individual job enrichment means to delegate to an *individual* a whole piece of meaningful work and to hold her or him accountable for the pre-established expectations. Meaningful work means that the individual totally utilizes her or his valued abilities and skills, which in turn have a clearly definable value-added impact. Individual job enrichment is an ideal situation (when possible) for an employee who is individually oriented in a high-involvement organization. A great portion of this employee's work design can be arranged in this manner (i.e., telecommuting). *It is important to understand that such an individual requires an exceptional attitude regarding personal responsibility, accountability, and empowerment, and is self-managed in terms of performance expectations.*

An individual who is given permission to operate in this manner should constantly be in contact with customers and management to know if he or she is meeting expectations and adding value to the organization's products or services. Examples of employees who may work best in this manner are artists and designers who create brochures and marketing concepts and materials, as well as individuals involved in research and development.

Work teams are also designed to have a group be responsible for a whole piece of meaningful work. Team sizes vary as a function of necessity for skills. Ideal team sizes are 4 to 10 members, although workable teams can be as high as 20 members. Team members must be (or become) social beings who are receptive to interpersonal growth. A major advantage of a team approach is that it reduces the need for management and places control in the hands of those closest to the work that requires improvement or change. A whole piece of meaningful work for a team is where the total process involves a clear input and output transformational process, i.e., something produced that is of a distinctly different quality from that inputted. For example, in an automobile assembly line, a team may be responsible for installing the entire electronics system, or a marketing firm responding to a customer's expectation may come up with a successful, creative sales slogan.

Team members require two major types of skills or training: technical and interpersonal. Without these capabilities, in addition to the four elements discussed above — information, knowledge, power, and rewards — a team will not operate effectively. *This means that an initial investment must be made in training and managerial coaching for work teams to achieve expected levels of performance.*

High-involvement teams vary measurably according to the amount of autonomy they have. Teams with maximum freedom are sometimes referred to as self-directed or self-managed teams. The basic rule is that a team is autonomous to the extent of its demonstrated or potential ability to perform (refer to page 90).

Management-oriented teams usually have a coordinating manager who serves as a coach and intervenes when the team is not functioning according to expectations. In spite of this mode of operation, these teams usually have team leaders within the framework of participative leadership.

The major rewards for both individual job enrichment and work teams are internal, such as job satisfaction, job control, freedom, creativity, and personal quality control. Very little in the way of additional financial rewards is associated with either of these concepts of expanded job involvement, except that in both situations, individuals and teams *are* rewarded for exceptional performance.

As products and services become more complex and there is a demand for shorter production times, there is also a greater need for work teams, even in cases where a single individual could perform the task alone. In fact, individual projects are becoming increasingly rare.

It is necessary that both the philosophy and practice of the organizational leadership are consistent with both of these high-involvement approaches to work. This objective can be accomplished by the establishment of senior management teams. These teams bring together senior managers in different cross-functional areas to plan more effective customer-focused strategies or to oversee the work of one or more teams which were previously supervised by middle managers.

Organizational Improvement Interventions

High-involvement organizations benefit measurably from improvement teams and task forces, particularly in their initial stages. As work teams become more empowered, there is less need for permanent improvement teams and task forces.

Audits and assessments to evaluate team and organizational performance are essential tools for benchmarking and continuous quality improvement. An Empowerment Assessment is a particularly powerful tool for periodic evaluation of the extent to which individual and organizational empowerment exist in an organization.

High-Involvement Management Practices and Procedures

- First, managers should continually seek ways to share information, knowledge, power, and rewards with employees.

- Routinely distribute all nonconfidential information concerning a business unit's operation to all employees within that business unit. The more everyone is informed, the better they know the big picture and make informed decisions regarding their work.

- Hold regular meetings with employees to constantly remind them of the organization's vision, mission, goals, and values. Managers should *live* the vision and *model* the values.

- Coach employees with the ultimate intent of delegating greater responsibility and decision-making authority.

- As employees acquire greater information about the organization's operation and more knowledge of their jobs, there should be a sequential process of delegating self-management of vacation time, performance reviews, scheduling, office coordination, budgeting, etc.

- Actively encourage technical and personal skills training as an integral part of the job. Managers should be the modeled example.

- Managers aspiring for advancement or greater responsibility should develop leadership qualities and skills in addition to management skills.

- Extensively include employees in all appropriate decision-making processes in a given business unit (participative decision making). As empowerment is gradually established, allow total decision making to be the authority of work teams and empowered employees.

- Provide acknowledgment and praise for outstanding performance when they are earned and deserved. These are valued by high-involvement employees.

- Encourage career planning for all employees and provide the opportunities for the experiences they require for their career plans.

- Establish direct links between employees and customers or clients.

Recognition and Reward System

The most adaptable pay system for high-involvement organizations is a *performance-based pay system*. In this system an employee is paid for her or his value-added knowledge, competence, and skills. This system is radically different from the job-based pay system characteristic of traditional hierarchical organizations. Performance-based pay focuses on the value added to an organization's goods, products, or services rather than on position or job title. Thus, it has the potential for creating career paths where there is no necessity for upward advancement.

As an employee develops multiple skills based on a solid knowledge base, she or he becomes more valuable to the organization. This individual is also invited to participate in a variety of work teams.

A performance-based system requires a high degree of self-responsibility, self-accountability, and self-management. It therefore encourages the learning of personal skills that go beyond technical competencies.

Although it was mentioned earlier that the primary incentive for high-involvement is not monetary, in some cases these employees may earn more pay than their immediate managers or supervisors.

Performance-based pay systems require substantial investment in training. A severe drawback is that there is no assurance an employee will remain with an organization after a substantial investment of time, energy, and money have been made in their development. In spite of this drawback, there appears to be little choice in whether to invest in their development. In the final analysis, an employee remains with an employer because of the overall mutual benefits they experience in *all* areas of work life.

Instituting a performance-based pay system involves:

- Identifying the tasks to be accomplished.

- Identifying the knowledge, competencies, and skills necessary to perform those tasks.

- Ascertaining the extent to which an employee matches these requirements or has the potential to achieve them.

- Increasing compensation as an employee performs her or his responsibilities at a high quality level with little or no supervision or guidance.

- A continuing increase in compensation as an employee acquires more knowledge, competencies, and skills which directly result in increased organizational revenues or cost savings.

◆ Designing a High-Involvement System — An Exercise

In the course of facilitating an organizational support system seminar for a major U. S. corporation, one of the tasks was to design a high-involvement system. The preparation for this project involved a combination of reading (see the bibliography on page 233) and practical experiences of utilizing people more effectively. The premise is that, given the opportunity and the expectation of self-motivated performance, most employees would respond positively. The seminar was designed to generate guidelines and behaviors in the three major areas influencing organizational operation — *structure, management practices,* and *work design.*

1)   **Organizational Restructuring** — What are some effective means of reducing our hierarchical organizational structure?

- Design a planned-level reduction process based on an end state of an empowered organization.

- Organize functions about the customer through cross-functional teams.

- Foster greater personal and team empowerment (through education, training, and transformation), reducing the need for management.

- Value and reward teamwork where managers become team members.

- Focus more decision making at the employee level, thereby reducing the need for management.

- Establish communication systems and networks between key individuals and teams throughout the organization (particularly those involving critical customers or markets).

- Focus on disseminating information regarding the big picture to all employees.

- Implement technology which gives employees greater access to critical information and opportunities to perform expanded job responsibilities.

2)   **Management Practices** — What are some management practices which *require* high involvement?

- The establishment and follow through of employee accountability where performance measures have been previously established.

- Responsible delegation, within clearly defined guidelines, with a total relinquishing of control.

- The unquestioned establishment of education and training as a value and also a required performance review criterion.

- The establishment of a mindset that employees are *expected* to be self-motivated, self-managed, competent, and learning continuously, as conditions for employment.

- Incorporate consensus decision making in group projects.

- Form cross-functional teams to perform whole and integrated work projects.

- Increase employee exposure to and direct interaction with customers; ensure decision-making authority consistent with job responsibilities.

- Implement 360-degree performance evaluations of leadership and management.

3) **Work Design** — How can our work be redesigned to achieve greater high involvement?

- Delegate stretch projects with clear accountabilities and facilitated coaching.

- Reexamine all present work processes for possible redesign or reengineering.

- Consciously shift from a management mindset to a delegator/facilitator mindset.

- Require staff to be responsible for a whole piece of work (a customer product or service) in a coordinated team capacity — with little or no management intervention.

- Design ways for individual contributors to be internal consultants to empowered teams.

- Create a work experience progression plan which brings employees through critical positions, decision making, and skills acquisition necessary for expanded participation.

- Establish a formal or informal mentor/sponsor program to foster employee professional development as management control is reduced.

- Incorporate enhanced information technology and offer training for necessary skills acquisition.

♦ Integrated Infrastructures

Most organizations that decide to implement empowerment have also begun or have been implementing other related initiatives, such as quality, reengineering, customer focus, and teamwork. In such cases, an empowerment infrastructure is best designed as an integrated infrastructure which includes principles and practices of the other initiatives. As we have previously discussed, empowerment is the anchor initiative which is common to all of the others in terms of *structure*, *systems*, and *practices*.

When the Texas Instruments DSEG division decided to establish an infrastructure for diversity, they immediately recognized its connection to empowerment and teaming. As a result, various members from each of the initiatives participated in a two-day working session to establish an integrated infrastructure which combined diversity, teaming, and empowerment. The fact that DSEG had won the Malcolm Baldridge Quality Award in 1992 added measurably to the success of this effort. That is, the process as well as the management and teamwork strategies were similar to those used in the quality effort. The other intangible factor was the enthusiasm of the participants, based upon the success of the quality initiative. They had actually *experienced* the value of a high-involvement initiative and its contribution to the bottom line. After the two-day session, a subteam of five participants developed a plan for implementation of the infrastructure, the resources needed, and the associated costs. This was a major step in having employees see the connection between these initiatives as well as bringing the diversity effort into their mainstream thrusts.

In the next chapter we go into more detail to show how the various high-involvement initiatives are related. In particular, we discuss the relationship between quality, empowerment, and diversity — where empowerment is viewed as the anchor initiative.

Chapter 14. Quality, Empowerment, and Diversity

◆ Introduction

This chapter is intended to show the relationship between quality, empowerment, and diversity. The discussion of quality is not intended to repeat the well-known tenets of quality, such as TQM (Total Quality Management). It is intended to focus on the mindset of quality which translates into empowered performance. The implementation of quality in terms of customer focus, teaming, and continuous improvement is what we define as empowerment. Diversity focuses on differences: differences in the way people are, the way people think, and the way people do things. The extent to which the expression of differences is accepted and encouraged is proportional to the extent to which empowerment is effectively implemented. Thus, we can begin to see that quality, empowerment, and diversity are interconnected — and possibly inseparable.

◆ Quality and Empowerment

Quality *begins* with a mindset which *anticipates* what best serves a customer, without the necessity of being told or the experience of breakdown. It requires a mental attitude of serving and learning which we define as a *quality state of mind*. This state of mind, in turn, leads to the most effective utilization of the quality techniques, methodologies, and metrics. Without this way of thinking, quality is simply a *process* of creating a never-ending sequence of corrective measures in an attempt to meet a performance standard. At best, this process is continuous improvement, but not quality as an institutionalized way of thinking and doing.

Serving

Serving begins with asking oneself two questions: What unique talents do I possess? How can these talents be used to bring value to others? Notice the focus is on others rather than self. When these questions are applied to the workplace, we might conclude the following: "I have a job because I have unique talents which are of value to my organization." "I am compensated because I use those talents to create value for a customer." Serving does not begin with asking, "What's in it for me?" Not that this statement is wrong; it is simply not what service is about. It also means that this statement and service are simultaneously incompatible. "What's in it for me?" will not lead to or sustain quality.

Once we are clear that we are employed to provide a service or product which is of value to someone, the next step is to discover how well we are doing. The obvious person to ask is the customer we are supposed to be serving. This is where the first difficulty commonly occurs. Many employees do not know who their customers are. This is not because of a lack of knowledge of how their organization functions or the people who comprise it. It is usually because the mindset of service does not exist. *Before* we can discover how well we are doing (which is the essence of quality), we have to know *who* we are doing it for and *what* they need. This is the point: we cannot serve a customer we have not identified and learned what they need. It follows that both of these questions need to be clarified in order to know one's level of quality performance. Although both steps might seem obvious, the actual value-added performance of them is predicated on a quality state of mind. This mindset is not so obvious, in practice, in many organizations.

I (BG) learned this way of thinking through a series of dinner discussions with my friend, Les Alberthal. In the early stages of our business, we had created what we considered

194

to be breakthrough processes in transformational learning — a holistic approach. When I explained to Les that I was having difficulty convincing a customer that we had come up with exactly the program they needed, he asked me why was it necessary to convince them of what they needed. If they truly needed it, the presentation itself should be convincing. This statement was confusing to me.

> An aside: Remember, confusion is a great place to be. It means one's present reality has been upset. Confusion often initiates an internal process which culminates in a different and often expanded way of thinking. Thus, it is a necessary part of the growth process.

He went on to explain that the customer is at the center of my activity and that the more I could learn to listen, the less convincing I would have to be. The key is not having to convince customers, but having them convince themselves simply by accurately providing what they want or need.

Learning

Learning is necessary to exist as a human being. It is a lifelong process. At this basic level, it is necessary for survival. At a higher level, learning provides the opportunity to live a more enriching life. For example, the more talents and skills we have, the more options and choices we have in life. From a personal standpoint, the more we know, the more enriching are travel and discovery. When the principle of learning is associated with quality, it is commonly because a customer wants a product or service which requires new competencies. It may also involve *anticipating* the needs of a customer because of a strong customer-provider relationship. Our receptivity to new learning is dependent on many factors, but most of all on our own mental attitude. We believe that every human being has some unique talent or ability in which he or she is capable of excelling. Living up to that capability in service to others is probably not a common attitude. However, this is exactly the type of attitude which has the potential to create a high-performing organiza tion.

When Marsha joined her new organization as marketing associate, she was very excited and enthusiastic. She had finally found an organization that embraced empowerment. This was going to be an opportunity to really show how talented she was without the control-type management she had experienced in two other organizations. She began work revising the company's brochure. However, she failed to talk to any external customers nor did she have firsthand knowledge of any of the consulting services her organization provided. The vice president of marketing played a hands-off role in order to allow Marsha the experience of working in an empowered manner. As the project proceeded to two-thirds completion, the vice president indicated to Marsha that the brochure was not quite the image of the organization. Marsha accused him of interfering and not allowing her to operate in an empowered manner. He explained to Marsha that in order to maximally use her talents, she had to acquire a knowledge base of the organization. She had to be receptive to continual new learning based upon an attitude of service. Although the experience was traumatic and emotional, Marsha realized that new learning was probably going to be part of every project. In making her decision to stay with the organization, she simultaneously experienced a shift in her attitude about new learning. Now she automatically assumes that learning something new — about the organization or an external customer — is always part of any project she does.

◆ Four Corollaries of Quality

If the quality of a product is synonymous with the quality of performance of its producers, then consistent, competitive quality is not possible without empowered employees. This relationship is summarized by four simple, yet powerful, corollaries of quality:

1) **Do it right the first time, every time.**

2) **Should it have been done at all?**

3) **There is no such thing as an honest mistake.**

4) **If it ain't broke, fix it.**

Each of these corollaries involves people to a greater extent than they do systems, although the two are *always* interconnected. In spite of the fact that most organizations view lack of quality as primarily a systems issue, we would suggest that the greatest contributor is the lack of appreciation or investment in the development of people — specifically, their personal empowerment.

Do It Right the First Time, Every Time

Do it right the first time is probably most identified with Phil Crosby. Although this phrase pushes the envelope, the title of this section ruptures the envelope. It is amazing how resistant we are when unreasonable but empowering expressions are presented — even when the new mindset has the potential to produce a truly incredible organization.

When the phrase *do it right the first time, every time* is embraced and practiced, it has the potential to change one's life. It does not mean that a person *never* makes mistakes, but it sets a new challenging standard that minimizes mistakes. For example, if a typist or computer specialist suggests to co-workers that no document or manuscript should be revised more than once after being typed the first time, this forces each of the co-workers to produce a more complete copy the first time, thereby reducing time, energy, and effort by both co-workers and the typist. It forces one to be in intimate contact with the customer *before* the product or service is produced, since doing it right means meeting or exceeding customer requirements.

Eventually this principle begins to apply everywhere in your life, whether painting the house with the utmost preparation, shopping with a well-thought-through list, or arranging a series of errands to maximize the success of each. Most meetings have to be held only once if the necessary preparations for time, information, and materials are properly handled in advance. This is a very powerful principle that forces one to more effectively organize his or her life and is obviously the foundation for life management.

Should It Have Been Done at All?

Should it have been done at all? forces us to stop and think about not only how we prioritize our activities, but about how we spend time doing things which are unnecessary (because of low priority or outdatedness) or could have been delegated through mentoring. The quality of our time could be more effectively utilized by asking three questions daily:

1) Could someone else do it?

2) Is it really someone else's job?

3) Is it necessary to be done at all?

One of the most common examples of this principle is the unchecked proliferation of paper, both in quantity of written materials or the length of a document; especially since we have laser printers. Another common office example is storing useless information in computer memory which will never be used or is of no interest to anyone in an organization. The memory storage is there; why not use it!

This corollary is perhaps best captured by the Pareto Principle which states that "80 percent of the important results in an organization are produced by 20 percent of the time, energy, and effort of employees." Where customer focus and reengineering exist, employees are continually eliminating outdated processes. One of the best ways to utilize this principle to derive the greatest quality usage of your time is to make a short to-do list daily, with each item prioritized in terms of "must absolutely do myself," "must mentor someone else to do," and "must delegate to someone." Ultimately, only those items in the first category should be on your list.

There Is No Such Thing as an Honest Mistake

There is no such thing as an honest mistake is a very challenging corollary, probably because most people *believe* there are honest mistakes which they feel they had little or nothing to do with. We do not *believe* this. Therefore, we do not live consistent with the unconscious expectation that honest mistakes will occur. What we are suggesting here is that what people believe, even unconsciously, frequently occurs. This corollary falls into the same category as the first one. It sets a standard that very few, if any, organizations attempt to live up to.

To get a better sense of what we are suggesting involves reminding ourselves of two important realizations of how life works. One, what you believe is what you expect to occur.

Two, belief coupled with expectation creates what happens in your life. Conclusion: if you believe honest mistakes happen, all you need do is retrospectively scan your life or, more importantly, your organization, and we are confident you will find a series of unfortunate incidents that could be understood by everyone as honest mistakes. Furthermore, you can be assured that they will occur endlessly in the future, with frequency!

Organizations that manufacture highly dangerous materials or that are involved in activities that could easily jeopardize the health of their employees, understand this corollary perfectly. They typically display large billboards publicizing their record of safety for "x" number of days. The objective is to create a safety consciousness which is to have its employees adopt a mindset that *through proper precautions, mistakes rarely, if ever, happen.* If you adopt this mindset, when and if a mistake occurs you begin to observe the incident as a valuable feedback source about how people and systems are working. Mistakes (even honest ones) are often indicative of necessary improvement in one of four areas:

1) Planning
2) Prioritizing
3) Procedure
4) Preparation

All four of these areas involve the performance of employees, not solely in terms of methodology and skills, but in terms of the efficient usage of time, energy, and effort. The invitation is to begin viewing mistakes, particularly "honest" ones, as feedback directing us to areas of quality improvement. The most common self-improvement areas are planning, prioritizing, and preparation. Procedure is the acknowledgment that there *is* a most efficient and effective system of doing things in an organization, which best fits the personalities involved. As always, the final measure is the quality with which internal and external clients or customers are served.

Another elusive aspect of this corollary is that honest mistakes rarely, if ever, *look* the same. They do not immediately reveal themselves as a pattern of general breakdown or relaxation of rigor in one of the four areas above. Only upon close inspection of a given mistake does one begin to observe something of a more *general* nature involving people or procedure.

For example, an excellent, producing employee who always appears to be overwhelmed and occasionally but systematically makes honest mistakes, may have fundamental difficulties in the areas of prioritizing and planning. His or her excellent output is often a veil which diverts attention from these areas of difficulty. Whenever a series of honest mistakes is examined and addressed in terms of one or more of the four performance areas cited above, an individual or an organization is provided the opportunity to establish a quantum jump in quality.

If It Ain't Broke, Fix It

If it ain't broke, fix it is a corollary which makes the basic assumption that there is *always* an improved way of delivering a product or service. Quality is a dynamic process of maximizing productivity and workmanship within the present time frame. This means that a quality product or service today will not be equivalent to the same quality of that product or service one month or one year from now. The slogan of an automobile manufacturer captures the spirit of this dynamic element: *"The relentless pursuit of perfection."* The first implication of this slogan is that quality is not a goal, but an ongoing process of improvement. The impetus for improvement is continual customer-encouraged feedback.

This corollary is a requirement in order to remain at the cutting edge of creativity. This attitude sets the pace for others to follow and usually mimic. In fact, the most revealing characteristic of an organization that is not operating according to this corollary is one that appears to copy what the quality organizations are *doing*. This practice may appear to work in the short term, but will *not* sustain quality in the long term. Quality, as a state of mind, is the source of doing things in a way that produces exceptional excellence. The *essence* of quality is not a methodology, product, or service. These are the *manifestations* of quality. It is vital to understand this distinction, or an organization will never achieve true quality as an institutionalized way of operating.

Quality involves encouraging, expecting, and training people to think a certain way about what they do. It appeals to something inherent in every individual, and that is the desire to express their full potential in an activity for which they have an interest and the mental and physical skills. This is the essence of empowerment!

The key becomes how to unblock the invisible barriers that seem to prevent such unlimited expression. We are back to education, training, and coaching as ongoing, integral parts of an organization's operation to ensure consistent expanding performance. We now understand that the most important part of this corollary — *if it ain't broke, fix it* — is the systematic process of *fixing* the creative potential of people even when it "ain't broke." The intent of these four corollaries is perhaps best captured by the following statement:

A mind once stretched by a new idea
never regains its original dimensions.

◆ Pushing the Limits of Quality

A quote which best summarizes the requirements for quality within an organization is the following from a *Business Week* magazine article, "The Push for Quality," June 8, 1987:

> *Managing for quality means nothing less than a sweeping overhaul in corporate culture, a radical shift in management philosophy, and a permanent commitment at all levels of the organization to seek continuous improvement.*

This quote expresses three important ideas which characterize a quality initiative:

1) Cultural transformation

2) High-involvement management

3) Continuous quality improvement

Cultural Transformation

The culture of an organization is the integration of its collective beliefs, attitudes, values, ethics, etc., which translate into accepted behaviors. It is a context dictated primarily by decision makers and policy makers and actively played out in practice by employees. Transforming a culture is like redirecting a ship. If leadership can find and operate the trim tab, transformation can occur with the least amount of effort. If not, it usually occurs with significant pain. Regardless of the exact method, transformation to greater employee responsibility and accountability will inevitably involve significant resistance. As we have previously stated, leadership plays the crucial role in minimizing the resistance and time duration until acceptance of the new reality.

Guillory and Galindo

High-Involvement Management

Quality, as defined by today's standards, most often flourishes in a high-involvement environment — an environment where those closest to the work play the major role in deciding how it is done within specific guidelines. The methodology of high-involvement stresses employee empowerment, teamwork, and focusing the entire company on the customer. This is a radical shift, even today, ten years after the introduction of TQM. The companies that are most successful are those which incorporate high-involvement into their business planning process. The most effective way to transform a culture is by integrating the change initiative processes into the mainline business. From a practical standpoint, it is equally important to show how the redesigned processes produce increased efficiency and higher quality products and services from a financial perspective.

Continuous Quality Improvement

Continuous quality improvement (CQI) is synonymous with self-improvement where employees view themselves as inseparable from the product or service they produce. Employees in this mode of thinking view this characteristic as a subset of the continuous improvement characteristic of an empowered employee. By making a dedicated effort on a daily or weekly basis to improve oneself, this improvement invariably shows up in one's product or service. For example, we both drive more than 25 miles back and forth to work every day. We listen to a full array of audio tapes — from business books to self-help to stories of Roman-occupied England. Quite often, ideas on these tapes trigger new insights about how to improve the organization's functioning or how to insert a Zen idea into quality improvement. The essence of CQI is synonymous with continuous self-improvement.

In an article published in the *Wall Street Journal* (October 2, 1991), Peter F. Drucker pointed out that major Japanese corporations were adding a new twist to the fourth corollary (page 201): *If it ain't broke, break it.* The new strategy was to begin the replacement for a new product the day it is sold to the public. And the way to maintain dominance in the marketplace while development of the replacement product occurs was to institutionalize zero-defect management (ZDM). ZDM establishes a higher level of quality than does TQM, which inherently has an acceptable level of error of 10 percent. If this strategy is successful, Drucker states, Japanese corporate leaders believe that by 1995 they will be ten years ahead of competitive markets in the area of quality. Motorola's Sigma Six program is obviously a response to this prediction. In essence, Sigma Six's ultimate goal is to achieve 3.4 defects per million.

♦ Diversity and Empowerment

Diversity is an environment wherein the total spectrum of differences is valued and integrated into every aspect of an organization's business operation. The extent to which an organization operates in the most empowered manner is dependent on how effectively systemic exclusion is prevented where employee differences are concerned. For this reason, diversity is referred to as the "people factor." Diversity not only addresses the issues of systemic exclusion, but also how to leverage the various dimensions of diversity as a competitive business advantage. Therefore, the overall objectives of a diversity program are to achieve:

1) *Diversity at All Levels* — Broad-based representation of all employees.

2) *Cultural Diversity* — A culture where diverse employees experience equity of opportunity in terms of practices, policies, and procedures.

3) *Diversity-Thinking* — An organizational mindset which views diversity as a competitive advantage.

4) *An Empowered Organization* — The maximum development and utilization of the total work force.

The ultimate objective is for diversity to become a permanent institutionalized part of the organizational culture.

Dimensions of Diversity

The various dimensions of diversity can be classified as *human, cultural,* and *systems,* as outlined below.

Human diversity is characterized by virtue of the physicality or life experiences of an individual. These include:

- Race
- Sex
- Differently Abled
- Marital/Family Status
- Sexual Orientation
- Ethnicity
- Age
- Military Experience

Human diversity principally involves the issue of human equality relating to the *presumed* inherent superiority/ inferiority of individuals based primarily upon physically distinguishing characteristics. Marital/family status and military experience are placed in this category because they are both permanent experiences which are always part of a person's life, even though they are not visible.

Cultural diversity is characterized by fundamental beliefs, attitudes, assumptions, values, and personal characteristics. These include:

- Language
- Learning Style
- Gender
- Historical Differences
- Cross-Cultural Relationship/ Communication
- Polychronic/ Monochronic
- Exempt/Non-Exempt

- Religion
- Work Style
- Classism/Elitism
- Ethics/Values
- Lifestyle
- Family-Friendly Practices
- High/Low Context
- Teaming
- Myers-Briggs

Cultural diversity involves issues of ethnocentrism: The human tendency to assume that one's culture and way of life are superior to others.

Systems diversity is characterized by the integration of organizational structures and management operating systems where differences are involved or implicit. These include:

- Teamwork
- Innovation
- Reengineering
- Strategic Alliances

- Empowerment
- Quality
- Education
- Corporate Acquisitions

Systems diversity deals with systems thinking: The ability to recognize the connections among different-looking systems and to be open and receptive to their *integration*. Of the three classifications, systems diversity is least recognized and consciously utilized as a diversity advantage. We cited team diversity in the various team descriptions in Table 1, page 90. We also acknowledged empowerment diversity when we encouraged the full use of the empowerment continuum in Figure 1, page 8. Therefore, diversity and empowerment are inextricably coupled through teamwork, productivity, high-involvement management, quality, and globally diverse cultures.

Teamwork

The extensive use of teamwork has become a fact of efficient organizational operation. It is the major implementation process in practically all high-involvement initiatives. There are two major dimensions to teaming: One, the unique way teaming is implemented, and two, the individuals who comprise the team. From a diversity perspective, we would like to focus on team composition. When individuals comprising a team represent a significant array of differences, resolving issues arising from those differences will determine how well that team functions and if it survives.

The following event illustrates how various dimensions of diversity unexpectedly showed up when a major computer chip facility attempted to implement teaming with no thought that diversity would be an issue.

We recently got an urgent telephone call from one of our clients. The manager of a manufacturing business unit indicated that they had purposely sought to create vertical as well as horizontal teams. What they had not paid particular attention to was the fact that the business unit consisted of 50 percent women and 50 percent men; 70 percent nonmanagers and 30 percent managers/supervisors; 49 percent minorities and 51 percent nonminorities; and 49 percent nonexempt and 51 percent exempt. Less than a month after implementing challenging but standard teaming processes, productivity was going down rather than going up. Finally, the highly charged but ignored issues of diversity cited above began to emerge. Employees who had all along harbored feelings of inequity began to speak out. The conclusion was obvious: The extent to which teaming would be successful was dependent upon how effectively issues of diversity could be resolved. We were asked to create a seminar which would help them resolve issues of differences, so that they could concentrate on the teaming effort.

This scenario is an example of situations which have repeatedly occurred in organizations as they have attempted to implement teaming while ignoring team member differences.

Diversity is the people factor. It must be anticipated so that the team's major attention can be on the implementation process.

When the differences between team members significantly influence the functioning of the team, we refer to it as a *cross-cultural team*. Cross-cultural teams include practically all of the dimensions comprising *human* and *cultural* diversity as outlined on pages 206-07. We have included human dimensions, since it is virtually impossible to rigorously separate culture from our human perceptions of people. For example, when we see a person of a different race or sex, stereotypes are immediately prompted, either consciously or unconsciously. It is important to understand that these stereotypes begin to influence our behaviors.

The diagram below illustrates the variation of differences as a function of team composition.

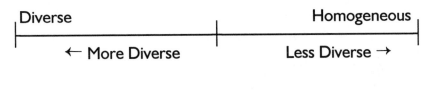

— Diversity Team Composition —

The further a team is to the left side of this diagram, the greater the diversity of the team. The more the team is to the right, the less diverse. One interesting observation is that there is no such thing as a purely homogeneous team. If two people comprise a team, by definition they are inherently different in some capacity. Two black women, two white women, or two Mexicans are examples of diverse teams where human diversity may not be a major issue. However, the ways these individuals process information and perform tasks may be significantly different. Therefore, we expand our definition above of a cross-cultural team by defining what we mean by influence. If a team has not addressed issues of differences, the influence will probably be counterproductive. If a team has addressed issues of differences, influence can mean that the differences are used for synergy and competitive advantage. This is the point: Issues of diversity must, of necessity, be resolved *before* a team can operate most productively. Therefore, diversity and teaming are inseparable.

Productivity

We define productivity as the quality and quantity of output per cost in a given time frame. By output we mean products, goods, or services. Two aspects of productivity are immediately obvious: One, the effective utilization of employees, and two, the performance capacity of employees as measured by personal empowerment. It is well documented that both women and minorities are underutilized in the U. S. work force. These findings are from surveys we perform in conjunction with our consulting as well as studies from various business schools. The underutilization of women and minorities is approximately 70 percent and 65 percent, respectively. This loss of productivity can be directly related to bottom-line earnings.

For example, an organization employing 15,000 women earning an average income of $25,000 per year, producing at an average of 70 percent capacity, results in a $113 million loss. In like manner, 9,000 minorities earning an average income of $25,000, producing at an average of 65 percent capacity, results in a $79 million loss. Making similar calculations for your organization creates an awareness of the connection between diversity and empowerment, as well as diversity and the bottom line.

The other aspect of productivity and diversity relates to the performance capacity of *all* employees as a function of expectations and development. If the beginning assumption is, "I don't expect certain classes of people to be fully productive because. . ." this can lead to a predictable cycle. The obvious managing behavior is to create experiences which fulfill one's expectations. This means assigning routine tasks, gathering evidence to support one's beliefs, and not coaching, mentoring, or developing the full empowerment of such employees. This cycle can be broken only by a nonintellectual recovery, acknowledgment, and ownership of the fact that we *all* have biased beliefs about other groups and classes of people. If we are not consciously working to change them, then by default, we are supporting them. *There is no neutral position!*

High-Involvement Management

Diversity is *the* way of life — both domestically and globally. It is literally impossible for managers and executives to be successful in managing without dealing with diverse groups of people. Remember, when we speak of diverse groups of people we are referring to dimensions beyond race and sex, although these two dimensions will continue to dominate the efforts in U. S. corporations. The diversity of workers is projected to increase dramatically over the next ten years and continue throughout the twenty-first century. In the U. S., the new *net* entrants into the work force from 1990 to 2005 will be 85 percent minorities, women, and immigrants, and 15 percent white males. From a global perspective, between 1985 and 2000 the world's work force will grow by 600 million, of which 570 million will be from developing countries such as Mexico, India, Pakistan, the Philippines, Brazil, and South Korea. Whether an organization focuses locally or globally, diversity will dominate the new brainpower in terms of both technical and nontechnical new workers.

211

Managers today have little or no experience in dealing with diverse groups of people. As high-involvement becomes more pronounced, so will the necessity for effectively managing diversity. Hierarchy involves more unchallenged management decision making, whereas high-involvement encourages mutual resolution and consensus for operational success. Therefore, today's managers will have to develop intrapersonal and interpersonal skills relating to the most pronounced differences represented in their organizations — both locally and globally.

Quality

Quality processes, products, and services are absolute necessities to stay in business or to operate an organization. As we have previously stated, quality begins with serving internal and external customers. Serving internal customers is related to internal processes and empowered teams (see page 90). As internal processes and empowered teams move toward greater self-direction, diversity issues naturally arise. The real key with respect to these two functions is a transformation of the organization's policies, practices, and procedures to provide equity of opportunity — cultural diversity. Creating a culturally diverse organization means transforming the culture to ensure the opportunity for exceptional performance by *all* employees.

The diversity opportunity, as it relates to quality, is viewing and using the various differences as a competitive advantage — diversity-thinking. Quality-improvement teams are provided the opportunity to take advantage of their diverse composition in redesigning outdated processes to more equitably reflect the natural motivations and talents of their people. In serving external customers, the most important change occurring is the acknowledgment of a diverse U. S. marketplace. Quality means providing these diverse groups

212

with products and services which reflect their cultural preferences. From a global perspective, the new emerging markets are even more diverse — Eastern Europe, Mexico, South America, Asia Pacific, and East Asia.

Global Cross-Cultural Diversity

The need for cultural diversity and diversity-thinking is already a reality for global operation. For many corporations, global cultural diversity has been a reality for some time. As more corporations make the transition from multinational operation to becoming truly global, new-looking diversity issues will begin to surface. A multinational organization is characterized by worldwide independently operating business units, whereas a global organization is characterized by transnational integration and alignment of strategy, structure, culture, and people. True globalization will begin to raise issues of global teams operating in cyberspace, global representation of the organization's executive leadership and board, and globally shared visions, values, mission, and strategies. Even though many U. S. corporations have been operating worldwide for many years, they have not had to resolve these issues within the framework of immense global cultural differences. This luxury will no longer be the case in the coming years.

Besides the unique nuances of doing business in a given country, diversity is the key factor in the successful operation of global teams. Avon Products, Inc. recognized the similarities of the countries comprising the Latin Belt — Italy, France, Spain, Portugal, Mexico, and the countries of South America. This realization led to a global marketing strategy which integrated the successful efforts from each of these countries. This is an example of utilizing the combination of systems diversity (teamwork) with cultural diversity (national cultures) as a competitive advantage. Table 3 matches specific dimensions of diversity with specific work-place applications. This table provides a guideline for using diversity as a competitive advantage. Although diversity is presently an opportunity for competitive advantage, as we move through this decade it will increasingly become a business necessity.

Table 3. Applications of Workplace Diversity Dimensions:
The Competitive Application of Diversity

DIMENSION	WORKPLACE APPLICATIONS
Thinking Styles	Creativity, Problem Solving, Systems Design, Teamwork, Work Redesign, and Quality
Work Styles	Teamwork, Systems Design, Work Redesign, Cultural Change, and Quality
Learning Styles	Teamwork, Systems Design, Sales and Marketing
Race	Sales and Marketing, Systems Design and Operation, and Creativity and Innovation
Ethnicity	Sales and Marketing, and Product Design
Sex	Sales and Marketing, and Product Design
Culture	Cultural Integration, Diversity-Thinking, Quality, Global Marketing and Sales, and Globalization
Right/Left Brain	Creativity and Innovation, Problem Solving
High/Low Context	Global Integration, Systems Operation, Marketing and Sales, and Quality
Polychronic/ Monochronic	Global Operation, Systems Design and Operation, and Marketing and Sales

215

Chapter 15. **Roadmap to Empowerment**

◆ Introduction

The following pages outline a flow diagram for achieving an empowered organization. We have modeled empowerment as a three-phase program. The first phase is *preparation*, the second phase is *implementation*, and the third phase is *nirvana*. Although we believe the sequences suggested for each phase are best for implementing an empowerment initiative, what is more important is that each element is achieved in the overall process. We conclude the discussion of empowerment by presenting the paradigm shift in thinking which will be necessary to maintain high performance into the twenty-first century — quantum-thinking.

◆ Preparation and Implementation

The elements of the preparation and implementation phases have been discussed throughout this text, with the exception of the Executive Leadership Assessment and the Organizational Empowerment Assessment in the second phase (see page 218). The former is a 360-degree assessment of each member of the senior leadership team. It is a self-assessment and a comparative assessment by their chosen reporting managers or employees. The results of the assessment are ideally presented and discussed as a private three-hour consulting session. The result of the consulting session is a plan for improving those areas perceived by managers or employees as requiring improvement. When this session is conducted by a skillful facilitator, the change an executive experiences can be profound.

217

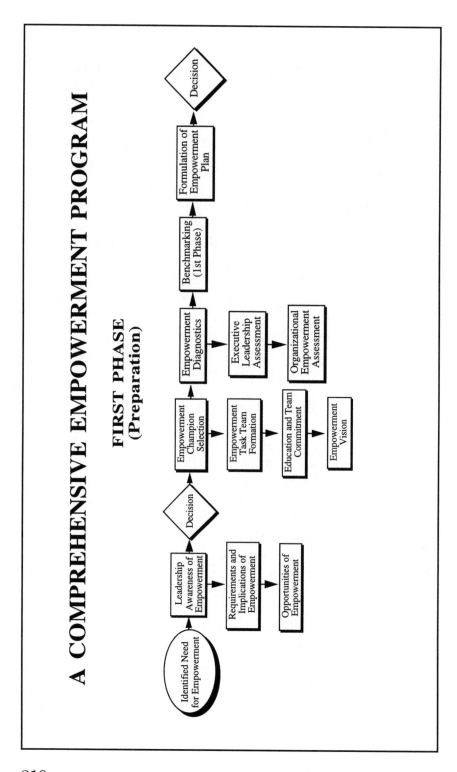

218

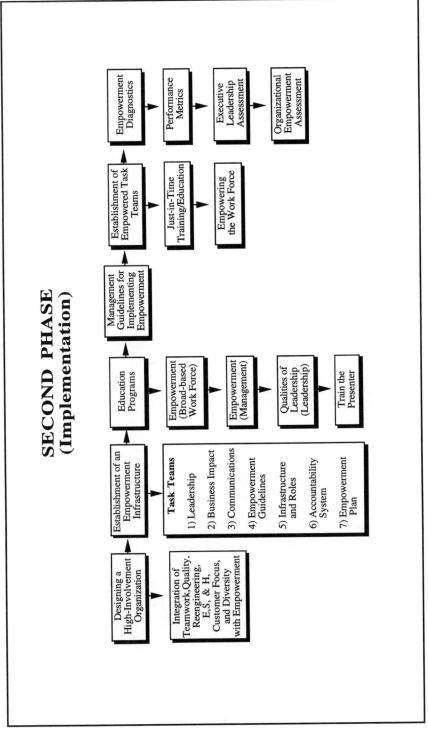

SECOND PHASE
(Implementation)

219

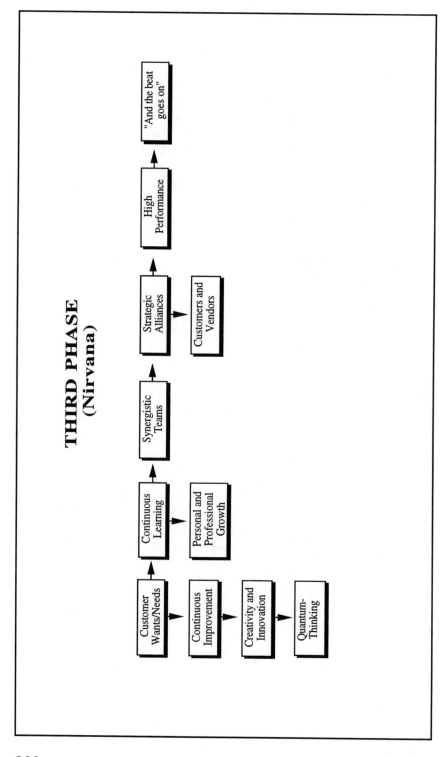

THIRD PHASE
(Nirvana)

"And the beat goes on"

High Performance

Strategic Alliances

Customers and Vendors

Synergistic Teams

Continuous Learning

Personal and Professional Growth

Customer Wants/Needs

Continuous Improvement

Creativity and Innovation

Quantum-Thinking

The Organizational Empowerment Assessment is an instrument which quantitatively measures the overall empowerment of an organization. This overall measurement is the average of the organizational support system and empowered employees as shown in the diagram on page 4. It is a quantitative measure of the upper and lower arrows in this diagram, respectively. This instrument also measures the personal empowerment of an employee, identifies the most important areas for empowerment improvement, and serves as a baseline for future measurement of expanded empowerment.

The sequence of the education programs cited in the second phase are respectively designed for the nonmanagement work force, managers and supervisors, and leadership. They are best performed simultaneously, but leadership should be one of the initial groups. This series involves the initial introduction to empowerment and how it is implemented according to the philosophy of this text. The other elements of phase two have been discussed elsewhere or are obvious by their descriptions.

Nirvana

Although customers are the center of attention in instituting empowerment in the first two phases, they also drive the cyclic process of phase three. Nirvana, as a description, is meant to characterize the ideal state of operation. When a new service or product is generated as a result of customers' wants or needs, the sequence of phase three is played out to institutionalized high performance and circles back to the customer wants or needs box — and the beat goes on. This cycle always begins and ends with the customer as the driving force for continuous improvement, creativity and innovation, and quantum change, either in meeting a customer want or anticipating a need.

◆ Quantum-Thinking

Eventually, the cycle of continuous improvement of a service or product runs its course. Forward-thinking organizations recognize that at this point the next-generation service or product is needed. A higher level of creativity and innovation is required than was necessary for continuous improvement. Organizations that discourage, *in practice,* creative and innovative employees are often *forced* into creating a new service or product or copying the latest service or product of forward-thinking organizations. Such organizations continually operate in a survival mode.

Achieving high performance (pages 23-26) is the *entre* into the game of business, particularly from a global perspective. The competitive lifetime of a product or service is becoming shorter and shorter. For example, the time to produce new software programs has been reduced from two years to 12 months, and is still decreasing. New management concepts used to last about five years; now they last about two years before a new concept is introduced. Information technology is being invented and applied at a dizzying rate and there appears to be no end in sight. At this writing, 100 MHz CPUs and quad-speed CD-ROM drives are state of the art. We are certain that within a few months they both will be standard equipment. In response, one question is, how does a business remain competitive? A more powerful question is, how does a business stay *ahead* of competition? The answer is *quantum-thinking.*

Quantum-thinking is the ability of the mind to function at a higher level of creativity. It involves a shift from information-processing, linear thinking to higher-order holistic thinking. *This shift to quantum-thinking involves the invalidation of the fundamental belief of the mind that its basic purpose for existence is survival.* It is achieved via an experiential, intuitive process, rather than one which is intellectual and rational. It involves the *nonintellectual* realization that, for the human species, survival is handled. In spite of this fact, we continue to behave in ways which are survival-based. For example, business is viewed by most corporations as a survival process of win/lose or live/die. In spite of the fact we can produce enough food to feed everyone on the planet, people continue to starve to death daily. We often live the expression, "this is a dog-eat-dog world," when, in fact, we feel the greatest harmony when we contribute to others.

The dominant theme in all of these examples is scarcity. *A scarcity mentality* is survival-based. Is scarcity *really* the situation? If the answer is no, then what do we really fear? The answer is change; because external change requires personal change for adaptation. The human mind, operating from a survival mentality, views change of the unique way it is programmed as a threat. The greater the change, the greater the *perceived* threat. The human mind makes no distinction between itself and the individual. Therefore, its survival is tantamount to the individual's survival. The true threat is not to an individual's survival but to the mind's resistance to changing *its* reality. Therefore, most of us change in significant ways only when absolutely necessary. The humorous paradox is, "the mind assumes that change is tantamount to loss of survival, and the ultimate reason we change is the necessity for survival." Thus, the breakthrough necessary to quantum-thinking is the shift from a survival mentality to a creative-adaptation mentality. This shift occurs naturally when one *realizes* that the major purpose of the mind is creative adaptation and on occasions physical survival is really at stake. This realization opens the doorway to one's unlimited creative consciousness.

Quantum-Thinking Requires Six Critical Skills

Quantum-thinking is achieved by the systematic development of six critical skills:

1) Personal mastery — the combination of a high level of self-actualization and professional competency.

2) Creative synthesis — the ability to transform information into new knowledge.

3) Intuition — the ability to access and validate spontaneous insights which are not rationally derived.

4) Context integration — the ability to see information and knowledge (contents) in several contexts and integrate those contexts to produce a new metacontext.

5) Hyperaccelerated information processing — the ability of the mind to process data and information at hyperaccelerated speeds.

6) Mastery of context — the ability to see the whole gestalt of a paradigm from fragment content, and function at a metalevel relative to that paradigm.

Organizations that capture, nourish, and fully encourage these characteristics in a critical core of employees will have such a decided advantage that competition will be the least of their problems. What replaces competition are cooperation, collaboration, and creative adaptation. Each of the six requirements for quantum-thinking are discussed below.

Personal Mastery

Personal mastery is the result of in-depth self-introspection coupled with self-motivated continuous learning. Personal mastery involves the willingness to move beyond any self-imposed barrier to discover one's *true* potential. The driving force for personal mastery is the continual desire for new knowledge and wisdom through continuous learning. Continuous learning is achieved by the absorption of new information *and* the creative integration of that information within one's existing knowledge base. The breakthrough experience to personal mastery is the realization and acceptance that change is not only a necessity but an opportunity for creative adaptation. Therefore, one acquires the confidence to create whatever is required at whatever level necessary, as a given.

Personal mastery begins with a fundamental shift in thinking and behaving which is typically the result of a significant transformative experience. Examples include a severe illness, the loss of a loved one, a peak experience, an in-depth workshop, or an existential crisis. In general, personal mastery appears to require a "rite of passage." The result is a shifted focus to accepting people and the world as they are. With this acceptance comes an overwhelming power to influence oneself and the events in one's life. Personal mastery, as with all forms of mastery, becomes a continuing process of expanded self-awareness.

For example, the fundamental learning that comes from earning an advanced degree is the acquisition of a discipline for navigating life. This discipline can be equally well acquired by the workshop of life — learning by direct life experiences — but more is required in terms of self-motivation and self-awareness. The better this discipline is learned, the more options an individual can exercise in life. For example, Michael Hammer was a professor of computer science at Massachusetts Institute of Technology before applying his thought process to the business world in terms of organizational reengineering. Personal mastery involves, most of all, a willingness to look within for discovering the power of self. The result of this process is the ultimate realization that, given the requisite professional competencies, an individual has the power to literally create her or his own reality. Practically every success story has these ingredients. It is difficult, if not impossible, to be involved with self-mastery without rigorously immersing oneself in introspection and self-awareness.

Creative Synthesis

Creative synthesis is the ability to create at a metalevel relative to the existing knowledge base. It is the ability to *see* interrelationships between a few apparently disparate parts. This ability requires an expansive base of information and knowledge. The critical experience is freely accessing one's creative capacity by the unlimited exploration of one's creative consciousness. The opening of this doorway is the key to the mastery of creative synthesis. Personal transformation is an inherent part of the process. The fear accompanying transformative change is the greatest barrier to mastery of this skill. As Picasso stated, "The act of creation is simultaneously the act of destruction." It is the destruction of one's presently existing self-limiting beliefs about reality.

This skill is learned by using an array of creative transformative processes. The creativity model used for these processes is based upon the assumption that the source of creative inspiration is beyond the mind. The true source of creativity is a universal creative consciousness. Using focused exploration, one is able to synthesize leading-edge

226

concepts from different disciplines to produce a new state-of-the-art product or service. For example, if one is attempting to discover how transformational trainings might be merged with information technology to create a product for mass utilization, the answer might be transformative multimedia learning. To create this product requires in-depth knowledge of human transformation *and* a creative ability with interactive multimedia technology. The new product is transformational computer-assisted learning.

Intuition

Intuition is the process of experiencing instantaneous perception of insight, information, knowing, or creativity. It is sometimes referred to as the sixth sense. Development of this skill is based primarily on trust in oneself. That is, the willingness to be cognitively receptive to the spontaneous reception of information with the least amount of self-doubt. The practice of "quieting the mind" is usually the prelude to intuitive perception. Each of us has a natural propensity for experiencing intuition in a unique way — by seeing, feeling, hearing, or knowing. And on many occasions we have! Depending on the nature of the intuitive insight, it must often be balanced with rationality before being put into practice.

The same doorway, so to speak, that one accesses for creative synthesis is also utilized for the intuitive process. The process occurs as though one is able to receive thought-forms which are subsequently brought to conscious awareness. The thought-form itself is typically preceded by provoking one of the human senses. For example, one may experience an instantaneous feeling from nowhere, followed by a complete perception that was not logically deduced. This complete perception integrates bits and pieces of data and information such that a complete situation is revealed, although total proof may be lacking.

For example, it is not unusual to have an intuitive feeling about someone's integrity or motivations, without proof, which is subsequently borne out. Equally common is intuitive visioning of how we perceive the future state of a product or an organization. This source is often the inspiration for a new entrepreneurial project or an organizational vision of the future.

Context Integration

Context integration is the ability to grasp the big picture with the least amount of data or information. It is the ability to perceive the whole system from the intuitive understanding of how a limited number of parts are interrelated. Context integration goes beyond systems thinking in that it involves an understanding of how a given set of parts or components can belong to several different contexts or systems. These contexts, comprised of similar components, are by definition interrelated. Thus, interrelated contexts provide the opportunity for the creation of a new superordinate context. This new superordinate context is the basis for a new breakthrough performance, product, or service.

For example, quality, empowerment, and diversity are each initiatives (contexts) for improving organizational performance. Common valued elements (contents) that exist among these three initiatives include: 1) people, 2) productivity, 3) customer focus, 4) inclusion and integration, 5) differences, and 6) teamwork. Since the three initiatives have these valued elements in common, they are *naturally* interrelated by a superordinate initiative (context). In this text, we have chosen to call this superordinate context a high-performing organization. The process of *integrating* and *institutionalizing* the various elements listed above is precisely the process of producing a high-performing organization. This relationship between different contexts with similar contents is a general observation, regardless of the specific example to which it may be applied.

Hyperaccelerated Information Processing

Hyperaccelerated information processing is the ability of the human mind to process data and information at hyperaccelerated speeds. This ability involves a combination of speed cognition and holistic knowing. Using this skill requires a knowledge base of the subject to which it is applied. It requires the hyperaccelerated integration of new information which expands one's knowledge base of that subject. Interrelated data produces new information and creatively integrated information produces new knowledge. As new information is integrated into an existing context, it necessarily modifies and transforms the existing knowledge base.

As a field (product or service) becomes mature, the continual integration of new information quite often results in the incompatibility of the new information with the existing context. The result is the spontaneous creation of a new context by a quantum-thinker. Examples are the transitions from classical mechanics to quantum mechanics, from classical music to electronic music, and from the information age to the knowledge-based age. The breakthrough experience in acquiring this skill is receptivity to the rapid accumulation of information without the necessity of evaluating how it might change one's present reality. The attachment to one's present reality is quite often the major barrier to mastering this skill.

For example, as we integrate high-involvement management practices into hierarchical operating systems, transformation of the underlying hierarchical principles (vertical structure, control, adherence to rules, etc.) will necessarily occur to produce flattened structures, greater freedom, and a relaxation of rules. The principle of this phenomenon is that "structure conforms to process." Therefore, the true reluctance to aggressively embrace high-involvement principles and practices is the attachment to one's system of beliefs, which equates to maintaining control. Control is a common belief most of us feel is necessary for survival.

Given the rate of change projected for the remainder of this decade, the ability to absorb new information as wholes will be a necessity to keep pace with systems changes. That is, change which is initiated in one part of a system ultimately manifests as significant change in an apparently unrelated part. For example, in order to address the economic situation in the U. S., we not only need to know how such an intervention will affect the economic situations in Japan, Europe, Canada, and other countries, but also the environmental implications of certain business activities, the utilization of a global work force, the radically changing U. S. work force, etc. It is necessary to accumulate an extensive knowledge base to be able to reasonably understand the operating systems' dynamics. In order to do so, hyperaccelerated learning is necessary.

Mastery of Context

Mastery of context is the ability to simultaneously be committed to a project and detached from the process or the outcome. It is the ability to be committed without investment. This skill is captured by the expression "being in the world but not of (or controlled by) the world." For example, if one is *committed* to creating the next-generation work force performance paradigm, one has to be totally detached from *all* the present popular initiatives. Once detachment is achieved, one can operate within or beyond the present paradigm in a centered manner. Literally any idea can be considered in presented or modified form in a way which focuses on the objective without regard to what presently exists. In general, the ability to operate "meta" to a paradigm is mastery.

This ability is perhaps the most challenging of all, because it involves *commitment without investment.* That is, 100 percent committed participation, *without* the necessity that a specific goal be achieved. For example, if one is committed to world peace, and every activity of that person's life is aligned with such a commitment, and world peace is not achieved in that person's lifetime, the achievement of the goal is unnecessary. That person's life activities would probably be a series of accomplished milestones leading toward world peace. This ability is also captured by the statement "spiritual leaders are people who *are* a difference" first, and by their leadership, they "*make* a difference." Being a difference means that a person is a living example of the difference he or she is attempting to make.

This is the point: More often than not, goal achievement is a given whenever it has commitment and alignment; although not always in the specific form planned. Detached commitment allows one to know clearly when an intervention is necessary and when it is not. In this sense it is a key element in adapting to and managing change — which is always accompanied by chaos. Detachment allows one to see the pattern within the chaos. It also allows one to see the fractures (forewarnings) which precede major change processes.

We can begin to see that the mastery of quantum-thinking involves, most of all, that we claim responsibility for creating our own reality. With recaptured responsibility, we can begin the systematic process of retraining the mind from survival-based programming to creative-based natural functioning. As indicated earlier, quantum-thinking *is* the future of globally successful organizations.

Nirvana Continued

The objective for empowered high-performance organizations is to continually operate in phase three. Following the flow diagram on page 220, the necessity to meet a customer need or want drives continuous learning. This learning may involve a personal expansion process as described in quantum-thinking or the mastery of a new technical skill. The attitude is one of receptive, dynamic growth. That is, life is a continuous process of learning, where feedback for improvement is a guide to engage the process. Then we begin to understand the Japanese concept of *kaizen* — continuous improvement through an attitude of voluntary, continuous self-improvement. *The process of self-improvement is synonymous with continuous improvement.* It is a process with endless milestones.

Synergistic teams were discussed in chapter 9. Since such teams and individuals operate in a self-directed manner, they are often in direct contact with the customer. The establishment of a committed long-term customer/vendor relationship is a strategic alliance. Such alliances require significant overlap of philosophies and values. They are alliances with a no divorce clause. These are established after a long period of mutual discussion and experience. They also begin to approach the Japanese *keiretsus*. Keiretsus are unwritten agreements where businesses work exclusively with each other, thereby, effectively eliminating free enterprise.

The culmination of the three-phase process (for the present) is a high-performance organization as described on page 25. This offers both the challenge and the opportunity for forward-thinking organizations for the remainder of this decade.

Bibliography

1) Harry S. Dent, Jr., **The Great Boom Ahead**, Hyperion, New York, NY 10017, 1993.

2) John E. Rehfeld, **Alchemy of a Leader**, John Wiley & Sons, Inc., New York, NY 10010, 1994.

3) Richard S. Wellins, William C. Byham, Jeanne M. Wilson, **Empowered Teams**, Jossey-Bass Publishers, San Francisco, CA 94104, 1991.

4) Joseph Campbell, **The Power of Myth**, The High-Bridge Company, St. Paul, MN 55114, 1990.

5) Michael Hammer and James Champy, **Re-engineering the Corporation**, HarperBusiness, New York, NY 10022, 1993.

6) Peter M. Senge, **The Fifth Discipline**, Doubleday Currency, New York, NY 10103, 1990.

7) Elizabeth Kübler-Ross, **On Death and Dying**, Macmillan Publishing Company, New York, NY 10022, 1970.

8) Robert K. Greenleaf, **The Servant As Leader**, Robert K. Greenleaf Center, Newton Center, MA, 02159.

9) Peter Block, **Stewardship**, Berrett-Koehler Publishers, San Francisco, CA 94104, 1993.

10) Judith F. Vogt and Kenneth L. Murrell, **Empowerment in Organizations**, University Associates, Inc., San Diego, CA 92121, 1990.

11) Edward E. Lawler III, **The Ultimate Advantage**, Jossey-Bass Publishers, San Francisco, CA 94104, 1992.

Empowerment Vocabulary

Empowerment is the performance capacity of an individual, a team, or an organization.

Management by Empowerment is a management system designed to optimize organizational performance through the extensive participation of employees.

Personal responsibility is the willingness to be the *principal source* of the results which occur in your life.

Personal accountability is the willingness to *own* the results which occur in your life.

Personal empowerment is an internally-derived capacity to continually perform to your maximum ability.

Delegation is the granting of authority with decision-making power within clearly defined guidelines.

Coaching is the interactive process of facilitating the expanded empowerment of an employee or co-worker.

Mentoring is the interactive process of overseeing and guiding the success of an employee or co-worker (and may or may not involve coaching).

Management/Supervision/Sponsorship is the process of overseeing the performance of a project or task to successful completion (and may or may not result in expanded empowerment).

A Commitment is a binding agreement with an individual or group to accomplish a task, project, or service.

Index

About the Authors

Dr. William A. Guillory is the CEO and founder of Innovations Consulting International, Inc. He has presented over 2,000 seminars throughout corporate America, Europe, Mexico, and Canada. He has facilitated seminars for over 150 corporations, including programs for the senior management of American Airlines, Avon Products, Inc., Eastman Kodak Company, Electronic Data Systems, Martin Marietta Corporation, Rohm and Haas Company, Sandia National Laboratories, and Texas Instruments.

Dr. Guillory is an authority on diversity and empowerment. He is the author of two books on personal transformation, *Realizations* and *It's All an Illusion.* He is also a member of NTL. His distinguished awards and appointments include an Alfred P. Sloan Fellowship, an Alexander von Humboldt appointment at the University of Frankfurt, a Ralph Metcalf Chair at Marquette University, and the Chancellor's Distinguished Lectureship at the University of California at Berkeley. He has been a keynote speaker for national and international organizations including *The International Chapter of the Society for Human Resource Management* and *The Institute for Management Studies.*

Dr. Guillory facilitates seminars on the following topics: — *Diversity; Empowerment; Creativity and Innovation; Qualities of Leadership;* and *Quantum-Thinking.*

Prior to founding Innovations, Dr. Guillory was a physical chemist of international renown, receiving his Ph.D. from the University of California at Berkeley. He has lived, studied, and lectured in England, France, Germany, Japan, Switzerland, Poland, and China. He is the author of over one hundred publications and several books on the applications of lasers in chemistry and was the Chairman of the Department of Chemistry at the University of Utah. Dr. Guillory founded

Innovations in 1985 following a period of intense personal growth which led to a career change to personal and organizational transformation.

Linda Galindo is the President and co-founder of Innovations International, Inc. She is a Senior Consultant and Facilitator and has presented over 1,500 seminars throughout corporate America. Ms. Galindo has been widely recognized for her outstanding presentations and her leadership in business. She was named as one of the top ten outstanding business women in the state of Utah by *Utah Business Magazine.* She has been recognized with an "Outstanding Presentation" award from *The American Society for Training and Development,* and was also recognized by the Salt Lake Area Chamber of Commerce with a "Pathfinder Award" for her history of work to further the development of women in business.

Ms. Galindo has facilitated presentations for over 100 hospitals and healthcare organizations, including VA Medical Centers, Brim Healthcare, Intermountain Health Care, and the Mayo Clinic, as well as Eastman Kodak, Electronic Data Systems, Trammell Crow, and Texas Instruments.

Ms. Galindo facilitates seminars on the following topics: *Managing and Valuing Diversity; Empowering the Work Force; Insights for Success; Responsibility, Accountability, and Empowerment;* and *The Human Aspects of Selling.*

Ms. Galindo writes a monthly column for *Network Magazine* on Personal Empowerment.

Innovations International, Inc.

Innovations is a global human resource development corporation specializing in personal and organizational transformation. We exist to provide the most advanced transformative technologies to corporations, globally, to assist them in prospering in the 1990s and into the twenty-first century.

Our specializations in consulting include:

- Diversity
- Empowerment
- Leadership
- Creativity
- Quantum-Thinking

These specializations include comprehensive consulting involving seminars, audits and assessments, coaching, and interactive multimedia learning.

The contents of this book are available as a three-part computer-assisted learning (CAL) program. The program features interactive multimedia processes including video presentations and scenarios, question and answer discussions, interactive case studies, and self-management skills.

For information regarding these offerings, please telephone, fax, or write:

Innovations International, Inc.
Woodlands Tower II
4021 South 700 East, Suite #650
Salt Lake City, Utah 84107
USA
Tel: (801) 268-3313
Fax: (801) 268-3422